THE
GOOD MIXER
COOKBOOK

A Treasury of Electric Mixer Recipes

By Diana S. Campbell

Dorison House Publishers, Inc. Boston

THE AUTHOR

Diana S. Campbell was graduated from Boston University with a B.S. Degree in Journalism, went for postgraduate study in home economics at Simmons College and took courses in education at Northeastern University. She now lives in Hanson, Massachusetts, and practices what she teaches — home economics in the nearby Rockland High School. Diana enjoys cooking, and is especially talented at making breads. This cookbook has many wonderful bread recipes, with illustrated instructions. Throughout, there are hints for success in baking and cooking all kinds of delicious food. The recipes were selected and tested in her own kitchen, and in consultation with Sunbeam's home economists.

Published by Dorison House Publishers, Inc.
824 Park Square Building, Boston, Massachusetts 02116
ISBN: 916752-49-6
Library of Congress Catalog Card Number: 81-69077

CONTENTS

INTRODUCTION

Newer, more revolutionary appliances are developed, but the electric mixer holds its own, performing functions other appliances can't. No other appliance can beat up egg whites or double the volume of whipped cream; no other appliance can produce the lightness and airiness so desirable in soufflés, cakes, pie fillings.

An appliance tucked away in a cabinet means wasted money. Keep your mixer handy, ready to work at all times.

Your electric mixer will speed your work in all sorts of projects. The tenderest, lightest cakes are possible as well as quickly combined cookies — even pie crusts. If yours is a standard mixer, complete with dough hooks, you'll soon find yourself a master breadmaker. Kneading done with your mixer saves much time, and produces finer textured baked goods. If you simply love getting your hands into the dough, knead by machine for only a few minutes, finish by hand. Not only will you spend less time, you'll be assured of excellent results. Dough hooks are also handy for those other jobs when you have to be careful not to overbeat, and can be used to cut in shortening.

Take advantage of your mixer's versatility. Stand mixers come complete with attachments that chop, grind, slice, shred and juice. The attachments are easy to store, easy to work with. Buy cheese in bulk, shred and store for casseroles and pasta dishes. Beat high food prices and use up all your leftover meats; ground up they make tasty sandwich fillings, additions to salads, loaves, mousses. Using your food chopper and slicer attachments for home canning will convince you of their worth. With fruits or vegetables scrubbed and ready, all you need is a large bowl into which everything accumulates. There is no constant emptying; just constant feeding; and you're done in no time.

Everyone is looking for ways to stretch the food budget and still provide delicious meals. Creative use of a mixer will help. This book has old time Sunbeam favorite recipes, together with new, everyday, economical recipes and fancier, celebration-type dishes. They are all designed to make quick work of your cooking and baking by using your electric mixer.

IMPORTANT SAFEGUARDS

When using electrical appliances, basic safety precautions should always be followed, including the following:

1. Read all instructions before using the Mixer.

2. To protect against electrical hazards, do not put Mixer in water or other liquid.

3. Close supervision is necessary when Mixer is used by or near children.

4. Unplug from outlet when not in use, before putting in or taking off parts, and before cleaning.

5. Avoid contacting moving parts. Keep hands, hair, clothing, as well as spatulas and other utensils, away from beaters or dough hooks during operation to prevent injury and/or damage to the Mixer.

6. Do not operate Mixer with a damaged cord or plug or after appliance malfunctions, or is dropped or damaged in any manner. Return appliance to nearest authorized Sunbeam Appliance Company service station for examination, repair or electrical or mechanical adjustment.

7. The use of attachments, not recommended or sold by Sunbeam Appliance Company may cause fire, electric shock or injury.

8. Do not use outdoors.

9. Do not let cord hang over edge of table or counter or touch hot surfaces.

10. Remove beaters from Mixer before washing.

11. Do not place Mixer or bowls on or near a hot gas burner or in a heated oven.

12. Do not use Mixer for other than intended use.

NOTE: The 350 maximum wattage rating is based on the food grinder attachment. Other available accessories may draw significantly less power.

Save These Instructions

HOW TO MAKE THE MOST OF YOUR MIXER

Sunbeam mixers have been making life easier for over fifty years. With constant experimenting, designs have now been perfected for the very best possible combination of speed, power, beaters, dough hooks, and bowls. Today your mixer does its job better than ever so you don't have to spend as much time in the kitchen as Grandma did. Just follow the instructions that come with your mixer, and you can count on it to save time and work and give you splendid results.

Reminders About Mixer Use and Care

- Keep it out on the kitchen counter where it's ready to use.
- Use a rubber spatula to guide batter into beaters — never a metal or wooden spoon.
- Keep liquid out of the motor.
- Keep air vents on motor heads open.
- Be careful not to overheat. When in doubt, use lower speed.
- Remove cord from outlet before cleaning beaters and motor head.
- Clean motor base and revolving disc with a damp cloth.

SYMBOLS USED IN THIS BOOK

At the beginning of each recipe in this book you will see the following symbols to tell you at a glance which Mixmaster mixer can be used:

Hand Mixer	All Stand Mixers	Deluxe Mixer	Power Plus Mixer

SUNBEAM MIXMASTER MIXER MODELS

"BURST OF POWER" MIXMASTER HAND MIXER

The touch of a special button gives you up to 25% extra mixing power for heavy batter.

**TOUCH
A BUTTON...
FOR INSTANT
EXTRA POWER**

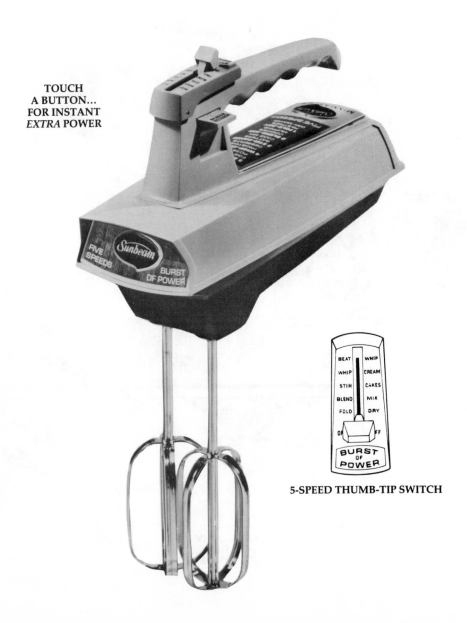

5-SPEED THUMB-TIP SWITCH

MIXMASTER POWER PLUS CHROME MIXER

This new Sunbeam mixer is the most powerful and versatile ever. Its heavy duty, 335-Watt governor-controlled motor delivers full power at all speeds. You can knead bread dough easily, and the deep bowls concentrate ingredients in the mixing area to mix thoroughly and evenly. The 16 speeds on the Mix-Finder dial allow you to select exactly the proper speed setting and eliminates guesswork.

**HEAVY-DUTY
DOUGH HOOKS
FOR BREADMAKING**

SPEED SETTING	MIXING GUIDE	EXAMPLE
OFF		
1	Fold	Use when mixing dry ingredients or when folding two portions of a recipe together, or when directions call for LOW speed.
2	Knead bread	Use when adding remaining flour to bread doughs and for kneading.
3	Stir	Use when stirring liquid ingredients or when a gentle action is needed to moisten dry ingredients.
4	Mix	Use when mixing dry ingredients and liquid ingredients together, alternately in a recipe.
5	Combine	Use when combining dry ingredients and liquid ingredients together at one time, such as when you begin making bread dough. See Breadmaking instructions for dough hooks.
6	Crêpes	Use for delicate batters, such as crêpe batter, when you do not wish to incorporate too much air into the batter.
7	Blend	Use for blending ingredients.
8	Cake mixes	Use when preparing packaged cake mixes or when directions call for MEDIUM speed.
9	Cream	Use when creaming sugar and butter together.
10	Whip potatoes	Use to whip potatoes or to develop a smooth batter.
11	Emulsify	Use when you wish to suspend oils in mixtures, such as salad dressings.
12	Homogenize	Use to make smooth, creamy mixtures, such as milk shakes.
13	Egg whites	Use when aerating egg whites.
14	Whip cream	Use to whip whipping cream or to develop a light fluffy texture.
15	Beat	Use to beat mixtures quickly or when directions call for HIGH speed.
16	Attachments	Use when operating any of the optional attachments.

DELUXE CHROME MIXMASTER MIXER

The powerful 235 Watt governor controlled motor of this model has been designed to keep on kneading — even through difficult mixtures, such as pumpernickel bread dough or fruitcake batter. It offers you a choice of 12 different mixing speeds, and assures thorough, even mixing with the bowl-fit beaters and bowls.

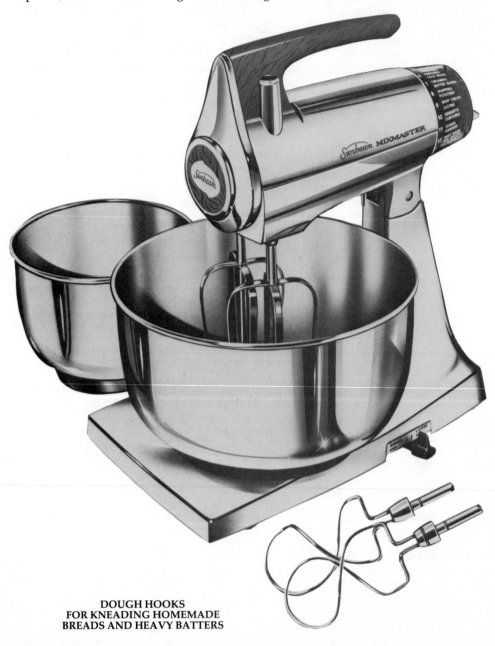

**DOUGH HOOKS
FOR KNEADING HOMEMADE
BREADS AND HEAVY BATTERS**

SPEED SETTING	MIXING GUIDE	EXAMPLE
OFF		
1	Fold	Use when mixing dry ingredients or when folding two portions of a recipe together, such as a beaten egg white into a batter or when directions call for LOW speed.
2	Stir	Use when stirring liquid ingredients or when a gentle action is needed to moisten dry ingredients.
3	Blend	Use when quick breads require a brisk action, just enough to blend ingredients but not enough to develop a smooth batter.
4	Mix	Use when mixing dry ingredients and liquid ingredients together alternately in a recipe.
5	Combine	Use when recipe calls for combining ingredients together.
6	Cake mixes	Use when preparing packaged cake mixes or when directions call for MEDIUM speed.
7	Cream	Use when creaming sugar and butter together; making salad dressings.
8	Whip	Use to whip potatoes or to develop a smooth batter.
9	Whip cream	Use to whip whipping cream or to develop a light, fluffy texture. Use with juicer attachment.
10	Desserts	Use to beat air into desserts such as custards and soufflés.
11	Frostings	Use when preparing light, fluffy frostings and candies.
12	Egg whites, attachments	Use when aerating eggs and egg whites and when using attachments. Use when directions call for HIGH speed.

INFINITE SPEED, MIXMASTER MIXER WITH STAINLESS STEEL BOWLS

This model has a powerful governor-controlled 175-Watt motor designed to perform any of the 12 mixing tasks shown on the mixing guide handle.

OFF
1 Fold
2 Dry Mixing
3 Blending
4 Biscuits
5 Cookies
6 Cake Mixes
7 Cream Butter
8 Puddings
9 Whip Cream
10 Whip Potatoes
11 Icings-Candies
12 Egg Whites

Easy to read mixing guide on handle

OPTIONAL ATTACHMENTS

DELUXE MIXMASTER MIXER ACCESSORIES ---

A. Disco-Chef Food Slicer/Shredder Attachment
The unique Sunbeam Disco-Chef Food Slicer/Shredder adds food processing versatility to Sunbeam's Deluxe Mixmaster Mixer. The Disco-Chef attachment was designed with the continuous feed feature for processing large quantities of food. 4 stainless steel cutting blades for slicing and shredding • Fine and serrated slicers — slice raw vegetables and firm fruits • Slices cabbage for coleslaw, potatoes for scalloping • Fine and coarse graters — grate pickles for relish, cheeses for pizza, bread crumbs • Convenient combination food pusher and measuring container.

B. Food Grinder Attachment/With Required Power Unit
Grinds all types of meats and fish from fine to coarse ground.

C. Juicer Attachment
The fast and easy way to prepare fresh citrus juices.

POWER PLUS MIXER ACCESSORIES

The versatile Sunbeam Mixmaster Power Plus Mixer has the power to operate these optional food preparation attachments.

A. Food Grinder
Grinds all types of meat, fish from fine to coarse — Stretches the food budget.

B. Slicer/Shredder
Slices and shreds potatoes, cheese and vegetables for salads, soups, entrées and desserts.

C. Juicer
The fast and easy way to prepare fresh citrus juice at home. Handy removable strainer included.

SUGGESTIONS FOR BEST RESULTS WHEN FOLLOWING RECIPES

1. Read the recipe completely before starting. The recipes in this book will be preceded by a symbol to indicate whether to use a hand or stand mixer.

2. Refrigerated ingredients should be at room temperature before mixing begins. Set those ingredients out ahead of time.

3. Preheat oven to baking temperature recommended in the recipe.

4. If directed in the recipe, grease baking pans with shortening, butter, or margarine, and dust with flour. (When using pans with a non-stick coating, follow manufacturer's directions.)

5. Measure out ingredients using standard measuring cups and spoons.

6. If recipe calls for "sifted flour," unless using presifted flour, sift flour onto a sheet of waxed paper or into a bowl. Then, measure carefully and sift again with other dry ingredients, if necessary.

7. When measuring dry ingredients, pile lightly into a cup with a spoon, overfilling the cup. Then level off with a spatula. Do not shake down into the cup or pack in tightly.

8. When measuring liquids use a clear glass measuring cup, and read at eye level.

9. Assemble all ingredients and utensils near the mixer.

10. To eliminate the possibility of egg shells or a bad egg in your recipe, break eggs into a separate container first, then add to mixture.

11. When mixing egg whites, be sure the bowls and beaters are thoroughly cleaned and dried. The smallest amount of oil on beaters or bowl could prevent the egg whites from reaching their full volume. Make sure no egg yolk gets into the whites, for this, too, will keep the whites from beating up into a foam. If some egg yolk should get in, dip it out with a spoon or a clean egg shell. To prevent this, separate each egg individually into a separate bowl.

12. Eggs will separate more easily if cold — do your separating as soon as the eggs are removed from the refrigerator. Then set aside to warm to room temperature — you will get far greater volume if the egg whites are warm.

13. After one or two minutes of beating egg whites, **soft peaks** will form. To test, after lifting the beaters from the bowl, the tips of the egg whites should fall over. If you are to add sugar, now is the time to begin.

14. With continued beating, the egg white foam will thicken. To test for the **stiffly beaten stage**, lift beater. If the whites stand up in stiff peaks, they are beaten sufficiently. Do not beat too long or your whites will become dry and brittle.

15. Some recipes require that egg yolks be beaten to their maximum volume. Yolks will not form stiff peaks, but they can be beaten till very thick, and a light, lemony color. To get to this stage, total beating time should be about six to eight minutes.

16. Follow the recipe, combining ingredients as instructed. If possible, use ingredients called for — do not substitute.

17. Use the correct pan size as specified in the recipe (see **Substituting baking pans section**).

BETTER BAKING HINTS

ABOUT HIGH ALTITUDE BAKING

Recipes in this book were tested for use at sea level. Changes are probably unnecessary for altitudes up to 2,500 to 3,000 feet.

SUBSTITUTING BAKING PANS

MEASUREMENT IN INCHES

Instead of this pan	Use this one
2 (8 x 1½-inch round)	2 (8 x 8 x 2-inch) square
2 (9 x 1½-inch round)	2 (8 x 8 x 2-inch) square or 3 (8 x 1½-inch) round
1 (8 x 8 x 2-inch) square	1 (9 x 1½-inch) round
1 (9 x 9 x 2-inch) square	2 (8 x 1½-inch) round
2 (8 x 8 x 2-inch) square	2 (9 x 1½-inch) round or 1 (13 x 9 x 2-inch) rectangle
2 (9 x 9 x 2-inch) square	3 (8 x 1½-inch) round
1 (12 x 7½ x 2-inch) rectangle	2 (8 x 1½-inch) round
1 (13 x 9 x 2-inch) rectangle	2 (9 x 1½-inch) round or 2 (8 x 8 x 2-inch) square
1 (8½ x 4½ x 2½-inch) loaf	1 (8 x 8 x 2-inch) square
1 (9 x 5 x 3-inch) loaf	1 (9 x 9 x 2-inch) square
1 (9 x 3½-inch) tube	2 (9 x 1½-inch) round
1 (10 x 4-inch) tube	2 (9 x 5 x 3-inch) loaf or 1 (13 x 9 x 2-inch) rectangle

MEASUREMENT IN CENTIMETERS

Instead of this pan	Use this one
2 (20 x 4-centimeter) round	2 (20 x 20 x 5-centimeter) square
2 (23 x 4-centimeter) round	2 (20 x 20 x 5-centimeter) square or 3 (20 x 4-centimeter) round
1 (20 x 20 x 5-centimeter) square	1 (23 x 4-centimeter) round
1 (23 x 23 x 5-centimeter) square	2 (20 x 4-centimeter) round
2 (20 x 20 x 5-centimeter) square	2 (23 x 4-centimeter) round or 1 (33 x 23 x 5-centimeter) rectangle
2 (23 x 23 x 5-centimeter) square	3 (20 x 4-centimeter) round
1 (30 x 19 x 5-centimeter) rectangle	2 (20 x 4-centimeter) round
1 (33 x 23 x 5-centimeter) rectangle	2 (23 x 4-centimeter) round or 2 (20 x 20 x 5-centimeter) square
1 (22 x 11 x 6-centimeter) loaf	1 (20 x 20 x 5-centimeter) square
1 (23 x 13 x 8-centimeter) loaf	1 (23 x 23 x 5-centimeter) square
1 (23 x 9-centimeter) tube	2 (23 x 4-centimeter) round
1 (25 x 10-centimeter) tube	2 (23 x 13 x 8-centimeter) loaf or (33 x 23 x 5-centimeter) rectangle

Chapter One
BREADS AND ROLLS

BREADS AND ROLLS

More than 10,000 years ago, bread baking started in the Middle East. Historians believe that the first bread was unleavened, baked by the sun. The ancient Egyptians are credited with making the oldest ovens ever discovered, and baking the first loaves of leavened bread. Bread was used as offerings to ancient gods, and bakers competed with one another to produce the fanciest loaves. Used also as money, bread and beer was all the slaves received as payment for building the ancient pyramids.

As the Christian era began, bread baking rose to an art, especially at holiday time, and fancy breads became symbols of national holidays throughout the world. Immigrants brought traditional bread recipes to the United States, and these old world favorites have become very much a part of our daily diet and annual holiday traditions. The most traditionally American breads are generally considered to be those made with cornmeal, since that was the most plentiful grain, most readily available to early American colonists.

Nothing can equal the aroma of freshly-baking bread. With many different types of flours now available, bread baking has boomed in popularity, becoming a creative adventure for the entire family to take part in. By letting the electric mixer do part of the kneading, you not only save time, but get a far more thorough job than that done by hand. Make good use of your mixer — you'll soon be presenting family and friends with crusty loaves of incomparable bread.

BREAD BAKING IN GENERAL

There are two basic types of breads, yeast breads and quick breads. Yeast breads contain flour, yeast, liquid, sugar, salt and fat. These ingredients acting together make the mixture rise.

Using the electric hand mixer, yeast breads can be made into a very thick batter, then poured into the baking pan and allowed to rise. This type of yeast bread is called a BATTER BREAD, and is never kneaded. A batter yeast bread has a coarser, more open-grained texture than a kneaded yeast bread. Batter yeast breads are quick to make, and retain a lovely yeasty aroma. This type of bread is ideal for coffee cakes, rolls, and quick specialty dinner breads, and is best when fresh baked. KNEADED YEAST BREADS are made into a dough which can be handled and shaped into loaves or fancy braids and rings. This dough has to rise before being punched down and shaped. Made this way, kneaded yeast breads have a fine, even-grained texture, resulting from the even distribution of gases, and full development of the gluten during the kneading process.

QUICK BREADS usually contain flour, a leavening agent, sugar, salt, eggs and liquid. They are quickly mixed together, put into pans and baked immediately, without having to go through a rising time. Instructions for these breads should be followed exactly, since overbeating, unless definitely specified, will toughen the end product. In the BISCUIT METHOD of making quick breads, shortening is added to the dry ingredients along with the liquid ingredients, using the dough hooks. In the MUFFIN METHOD, all the dry ingredients are very quickly stirred into the liquid ingredients, using a very low mixer speed and, in some recipes, the dough hooks. Be very careful to follow recipe directions exactly and do not over-beat.

SUCCESS HINTS

FLOUR

In order to make a good loaf of yeast bread, **gluten** must be present in the flour used. Gluten, found in wheat flour, is the ingredient which makes the texture and elasticity of the bread. Generally, the most commonly available flour is all-pur-pose, bleached or unbleached. There is no difference in the texture of bread made with either type — one might prefer the color of the bread made with unbleached flour.

Once you have mastered the art of baking a good loaf of bread, you will want to ex-periment with the various types of grains and special flours now available to the home baker, such as stone-ground flours and meals, buckwheat or graham flour.

Keep in mind maximum amounts of flour to be used when kneading bread with your Sunbeam Mixmaster Mixer. Consult the general Bread Making Tips to be sure you do not exceed this maximum.

YEAST

Yeast is a living plant which, when activated, produces carbon dioxide gas. This causes the dough to rise. Excessively high heat kills yeast, which is why tempera-ture is of great importance in bread baking. Ideal growing temperature for yeast is 80-85° F.

Two types of yeast are available, **Active Dry Yeast and Compressed Yeast.** Com-pressed yeast must be stored in the refrigerator, and used within two weeks. Ac-tive dry yeast is also best stored in the refrigerator. It comes in packages contain-ing about one tablespoon of dry yeast, and also comes in 4-ounce jars. The expira-tion date is marked on the outside of the package or jar. If you should buy yeast that does not have a date on it, be sure to **proof** it before mixing the bread, to be sure it is still active. Compressed yeast is dissolved in liquid no warmer than 95° F. while active dry yeast takes a slightly warmer temperature of 110-115° F. For best results, use a thermometer, especially if you are a novice, until you get used to how warm the liquid feels to the touch, or when sprinkled on the inside of your wrist.

To **proof** yeast, which will indicate to you that the yeast is active, use ¼ to ½ cup of warm water, stirring in the yeast and a teaspoon of sugar. If water is not called for in your recipe, substitute a half cup of water for part of the liquid used in the reci-pe; yeast dissolves better in water than it does in milk. The sugar provides food for the yeast, and will cause it to bubble and grow in the cup. If it does not do this, you will know that your yeast is probably too old, or that the water you used is too hot.

LIQUID

Milk and water are the two basic liquids used in bread making. Water will produce a crisper crust, milk produces a smoother textured loaf, with browner crust. Do not hesitate to use dry milk in bread making. Add the dry milk solids with the flour, and use water for the liquid — no need to reconstitute the milk beforehand.

OTHER INGREDIENTS

Besides adding flavor, sugar provides food for the yeast to grow. Salt regulates the rising of the dough — measure carefully, for too much salt can reduce action of the yeast. Any type of fat can be used in bread, depending on the flavor desired. Fat also tenderizes and improves keeping quality of the bread.

COMBINING THE INGREDIENTS

The first steps in bread making, before final addition of flour, can be made with a portable hand mixer, such as the Sunbeam Power Plus or Intermediate Mixer.

BE SURE TO CHECK PROPER SPEED SETTINGS FOR ALL MODELS AS INDICATED IN CHARTS IN THE BEGINNING OF THIS BOOK AND THE INSTRUCTION BOOK WHICH ACCOMPANIED YOUR MIXER.

The **Rapidmix** method of bread making makes the entire mixing procedure easier, while saving time. With this method, you combine one-third of the flour and the dry yeast; gradually add the warm liquid, shortening, sugar and salt, beating at medium speed, using the regular beaters. Add eggs, and about a half cup of flour and beat at high speed for two more minutes. This much can be done with your hand mixer; the rest of the flour can be stirred in using a spoon. Knead by hand or insert dough hooks, add remainder of the flour, and let your mixer do the kneading.

The **Coolrise** method of breadmaking was developed for those who do not have the time to follow through the entire breadmaking process at one time. The bread is made much the same way as the Rapidmix method, then given a "resting" period of twenty minutes. The dough is punched down, loaves shaped, and the pans refrigerated for two to 24 hours, when the dough will rise. This eliminates the entire first rising in the conventional method of breadmaking. Coolrise recipes should be followed closely; the Rapidmix method can be substituted for most yeast bread recipes.

When kneading bread with doughhooks, using your Sunbeam Mixmaster deluxe mixer or Mixmaster Power Plus, do not use recipes calling for total amounts of flour greater than the following:

Deluxe Mixmaster Mixer	3½-4 cups flour
Power Plus Mixmaster Mixer	5½-6 cups flour

When making kneaded breads, your mixer will require more care than when making ordinary mixtures, such as cake batter and cookie dough. The elasticity of the bread dough and the shape of the dough hooks may cause your mixer to do some unusual things. The mixer head may rock up and down. Don't be alarmed. This action is normal. DO NOT ATTEMPT TO HOLD THE MIXER HEAD DOWN, AS THIS MAY INTERFERE WITH THE KNEADING ACTION.

The bowl may tend to rock back and forth or be slow in starting to rotate. We suggest that you guide the bowl with one hand to help control the rocking action or to start its rotating. Don't get your hands too near the dough hooks!

The kneading action may cause the mixer to slide on a slippery work surface. Be sure the work surface and rubber feet on the bottom of the mixer are clean and dry.

CAUTION: Do not use the mixer too near the edge of a table or counter top, where it could fall off.

Ingredients should be added to the mixing bowl as they are specified in the recipe.

Combine a small portion of the dry ingredients with the wet ingredients. Start mixing on a slightly higher speed (Speed 3 to 5). Continue adding dry ingredients until the mixture becomes sticky, then turn to Speed 1 or 2. Gradually add remaining dry ingredients.

Note: While you are working with a liquid mixture your mixer, with dough hooks inserted, can be operated at a high speed. After addition of final amount of flour, your dough hooks are **not** made to operate at a high speed. Be very certain to use recommended kneading speed for your particular model — consult the chart for proper kneading speed.

If there is high humidity in the air, it may be necessary to add additional flour to the recipe; high humidity could also extend the amount of time necessary for baking. Be careful not to add too much flour — you want a soft dough.

If you live in a high altitude area, yeast breads will require a shorter rising time. Allow the dough to rise only until it has doubled in size. Slightly less flour should be used because the flour is dryer at higher altitudes.

Do not attempt to feed dough into the dough hooks with your hands. Use a spatula, or any other utensil, while the mixer is plugged into an outlet or is in operation. Should an object, such as a spatula, fall into the bowl while the mixer is operating, turn the mixer OFF immediately. Then remove the object.

When mixing or kneading is complete, turn the Mix-Finder dial to OFF. Raise the mixer head. Use a rubber or plastic spatula to scrape excess dough from the dough hooks. Remove dough hooks and place in sink for easy clean-up.

DOUGH RISING TIPS

Use a well-greased, large bowl for the first rising. Gather up the ball of kneaded dough and place it in the bowl and cover with a light cloth. Place in a draft-free, warm area such as a cool oven, with a pan of hot water on the lower shelf. The best temperature is 80-85° F.

Be sure that the dough rises to double in volume. A reliable test to check the dough when it looks ready is to make an indentation in it with two fingers. If the dough DOES NOT spring back, it is ready. **Note:** Do not use this test once the dough has been shaped into loaves.

To punch down dough, plunge fist into center of risen dough, to punch out large air bubbles, and bring in a new supply of oxygen to the dough. Fold outer edges over into center.

Dough should be shaped according to directions, and put into prepared pans. For the second rising, treat the dough as you did the first time, covering the pans and placing them in the warm place.

How to shape dough for a loaf pan:

1. Sprinkle dough lightly with flour.

2. Using a rolling pin, roll dough into a rectangle.

3. Roll dough into a loaf, starting from narrow end.

4. Flatten ends with sides of hands, as shown.

5. Pinch along seam to seal.

6. Fold ends under and place seam-side down in a well-greased loaf pan.

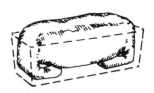

Bake in preheated oven. To test for doneness, when the loaf appears to be done, tap it with your knuckles. If it sounds hollow, turn it into a towel, bottom up. Tap the bottom of the loaf with your finger. If it sounds hollow, and the bottom seems crisp and done, remove to a cooling rack. If the bottom is very soft, return to pan and continue baking. You can make the bottom crust crisper by placing the bread directly on the oven rack to bake for just a couple of minutes.

Leave the loaf as it is, on a cooling rack, for a crisp crust. If a tender crust is desired, brush tops of loaves with melted butter upon removal from the oven. If you'd like your loaves to have a shiny glaze, slightly beat an egg and add one tablespoon of water. Brush this glaze over tops of loaves BEFORE baking.

Bake an extra loaf of bread and freeze it. Be sure to wrap the bread properly for the freezer. First be certain that the loaf has cooled completely, then wrap snugly in plastic freezer wrap or aluminum foil, making an airtight package. The smallest amount of air will dry out your loaf. Properly wrapped, most bread keeps well frozen up to six months.

WHITE BREAD   Yield: 1 loaf

½ cup milk
2 tablespoons butter or margarine
1 tablespoon plus 1 teaspoon
   granulated sugar

1 teaspoon salt
1 package active dry yeast
¾ cup warm water (110-120° F.)
3¼ cups sifted all-purpose flour,
   divided

Insert dough hooks into mixer. Grease a large, glass bowl and set aside. Scald milk and then add butter, sugar, and salt. Cool to room temperature. In a large mixing bowl, dissolve yeast in warm water. Add 1 cup flour and milk mixture. Mix on medium speed until well blended. Add 1¼ cups flour and continue mixing until well blended. Scrape sides of bowl, as necessary. Turn to knead and gradually add remaining 1 cup flour. Continue kneading until flour has been thoroughly combined. Total mixing/kneading time should be 6-8 minutes. Form into a ball and roll the ball to grease the dough. Cover and let rise until double in bulk, about 90 minutes. Punch down dough. Allow to rise until doubled, about 40 minutes. Punch down, remove from bowl, and let rest on a lightly floured board for 10 minutes. Meanwhile, grease a 9x5x3-inch loaf pan. Form into a loaf and place in prepared pan. Cover and allow to rise until doubled, about 30 minutes. Preheat oven to 375° F. Bake for 40-50 minutes, or until done.

OLD-FASHIONED WHITE BREAD   Yield: 2 loaves

The addition of eggs makes nice color and flavor — extra nourishing, too!

5-5½ cups all-purpose flour
2 packages active dry yeast
3 tablespoons granulated sugar
2 teaspoons salt

2 cups warm water
1 cup dry skim milk powder
2 eggs
3 tablespoons vegetable oil

Insert dough hooks. Using low speed, stir together 2½ cups flour, yeast, sugar or honey, salt and powdered milk. Gradually add warm water. Continue beating 3-4 minutes, turning mixer up to medium speed. Beat in eggs and oil. Turn mixer to proper kneading speed and add remaining flour. Scrape sides of bowl as necessary. Knead dough 3-5 minutes, or until it forms a soft ball of dough. Cover and place in a warm, draft-free place to rise until double, about 1 hour. Punch down and shape into loaves. Allow to rise until double, about 1 hour. Brush loaves with melted butter. Bake in preheated oven 375° F. for about 35-40 minutes.

Cut in half for use with Deluxe Mixmaster Mixer.

100% WHOLE WHEAT BREAD   Yield: 2 loaves

An extra step to this bread — well worth the time.

2½ cups whole wheat flour
½ cup dry milk powder
1 package active dry yeast

1½ cups warm water
⅓ cup honey or brown sugar

Combine the ingredients in a large mixer bowl. Beat at medium speed 3-4 minutes. Cover and let batter rise in a warm place for 1 hour. Stir down the batter, insert dough hooks, and add:

2 teaspoons salt
¼ cup vegetable oil

1½-2 cups whole wheat flour
1 egg

Knead at recommended speed for 6-8 minutes. Put dough in well-greased bowl, and roll the ball to grease the dough. Cover and put on a warm, draft-free place to rise until double in bulk. Punch down and shape into loaves. Let rise until double. Preheat oven to 350° F. Bake loaves 50-60 minutes.

Cut in half for Deluxe Mixmaster Mixer.

OATMEAL BREAD   Yield: 2 loaves

1 cup milk
1 cup water
4 tablespoons margarine or butter
1 cup rolled oats

1 teaspoon salt
½ cup molasses
2 packages active dry yeast
4½ to 5 cups all-purpose flour

In medium sauce pan combine milk, water and shortening and bring to boil. Stir in oatmeal and immediately remove from heat. Set aside to cool to lukewarm. Pour into large mixer bowl; add salt, molasses and yeast. Insert dough hooks and beat at medium speed for 2 minutes. At low speed, knead in flour, kneading in enough to make a smooth, soft, elastic dough which does not cling to the sides of the bowl. Total mixing/kneading time should be 6-8 minutes.

Put dough in large greased bowl, and roll the ball to grease the dough. Cover and put in warm place to rise until doubled in bulk, 1-1½ hours. Punch down. Divide in half, form into loaves and put into 2 greased 9-inch loaf pans. Let rise until double. Preheat oven to 375° F. and bake about 40 minutes or until done.

FRENCH BREAD   Yield: 1 loaf

1 package active dry yeast
1 cup warm water (110-120°F.)
1½ teaspoons granulated sugar
1 teaspoon salt

2¾ cups all-purpose flour, divided
¼ cup yellow cornmeal
2 tablespoons salad oil

Insert dough hooks into mixer. Grease a large, glass bowl and set aside. In a large mixing bowl, dissolve yeast in warm water. Add sugar, salt and 1 cup flour to yeast mixture. Mix on medium speed until well blended. Gradually add 1 cup flour. Scrape sides of bowl as necessary. Turn to knead and gradually add remaining ingredients kneading until flour has been thoroughly combined. Total mixing/ kneading time should be 6-8 minutes. Remove dough from mixing bowl. Form into a ball and cool the ball to grease the dough. Cover and let rise 90 minutes. Punch down, remove from bowl, and let rest on a lightly floured board for 10 minutes. Dust an ungreased cooking sheet with cornmeal. Form dough into a long loaf and place on cooking sheet. Slash top of loaf with sharp knife. Cover and allow to rise 90 minutes. Preheat oven to 375° F. Brush loaf lightly with salad oil. Bake for 40-50 minutes.

SALLY LUNN BREAD   Yield: 1 loaf

1 package dry yeast
½ cup warm water (105-115° F.)
½ cup warm milk
½ cup butter or margarine, softened

⅓ cup granulated sugar
3 eggs, well beaten
3½ cups all-purpose flour
1 teaspoon salt

Combine yeast and water in a small bowl; set aside for 5 minutes. Stir in milk. In large mixing bowl, cream butter and sugar on high speed until light and fluffy — about 1 minute. Add eggs, blending well. Turn to low speed. Combine flour and salt; add to creamed mixture alternately with milk mixture, beginning and ending with flour. Mix well after each addition. Cover and let rise in a warm place (85° F.), free from drafts, about 2 hours or until doubled in bulk. Spoon batter into a well-greased 10-inch tube pan or Bundt pan. Cover and let rise in a warm place, free from drafts, until doubled in bulk. Bake at 350° F. for 50-60 minutes. (Bread is done when toothpick inserted in center of bread comes out clean.) Remove from pan; cool on wire rack.

PUMPERNICKEL RYE BREAD   Yield: 1 loaf

1 package active dry yeast
¼ cup warm water
¼ cup cornmeal
¾ cup water
1 teaspoon sugar
3 tablespoons molasses
1½ teaspoon salt
1 tablespoon butter or margarine

1½ teaspoons caraway seeds
1 cup instant mashed potatoes
    (prepared as per package
    directions)
1 cup rye flour
1 cup whole wheat flour
1¼ cups all-purpose flour

Insert dough hooks into mixer. Cook cornmeal in ¾ cup water. Stir in molasses, margarine, salt, caraway seeds, and potatoes. Cool to lukewarm. In large mixing bowl dissolve yeast in ¼ cup water; add sugar. Add warm cornmeal mixture to yeast. Combine all flours. Add 2 cups flour mixture. Thoroughly combine ingredients on low speed for ½ minute. Turn to medium speed, process for ½ minute. Stop mixer; add 1¼ cups flour mixture. Mix and knead on low speed for 2 minutes. Place dough into greased bowl and let rise 90 minutes. Punch dough down. Let rise 40 minutes. Punch down again and place on a floured board to rest 10 minutes. Shape into a loaf and place into a greased 9 × 5 x 3-inch baking pan. Allow to rise 30 minutes. Bake in a 375° F. oven for 50 minutes. Baked loaf will sound hollow when tapped with knuckles.

COOLRISE FRENCH BREAD   Yield: 2 loaves

5½-6½ cups all-purpose flour
2 packages active dry yeast
1 tablespoon granulated sugar
1 tablespoon salt

2 tablespoons shortening
2¼ cups very warm water
Cooking oil

Insert dough hooks. In large mixer bowl, combine 2 cups flour, yeast, sugar and salt. Stir at low speed about 30 seconds to blend. Add shortening, then very warm water. Turn mixer to medium speed and beat for 2 minutes, scraping bowl often. Add 1 more cup of flour, turn to high speed and beat 1 minute or until very thick and elastic. Turn mixer to knead and add enough remaining flour to make a soft dough which cleans the sides of the bowl. Total mixing/kneading time should be 6-8 minutes. Dough should be very smooth and elastic. Place on lightly floured board; cover with plastic wrap, then a towel, and allow to rest for 20 minutes. Punch down and divide in half. Shape into 2 long loaves on a large greased baking sheet. Brush dough lightly with oil and cover with plastic wrap (wrap loosely so that loaves have room to rise). Refrigerate 2-24 hours. Remove from refrigerator 10 minutes before baking. Preheat oven to 400° F. and bake loaves 30-40 minutes or until they test done. Cool on racks.

Note: Recipe can be halved to make 1 loaf. Just be certain to use half the amount of flour in each of the beating steps.

COOLRISE WHITE BREAD   Yield: 2 loaves

5½-6½ cups all- purpose flour
2 packages active dry yeast
2 tablespoons granulated sugar
1 tablespoon salt

3 tablespoons margarine
1¾ cups milk
½ cup water
Cooking oil

Insert dough hooks. In large mixer bowl combine 2 cups flour, yeast, sugar and salt. Stir at low speed about 30 seconds to blend. Add margarine and milk and water which have been heated till warm (115° F.-120° F.). Beat at medium speed for 2 minutes, scraping bowl occasionally. Add 1 more cup flour and beat at high speed for 1 minute or until very thick and elastic. Turn mixer to knead and gradually add enough more flour to form a soft dough which cleans the sides of the bowl. Total mixing/kneading time will be 6-8 minutes. Turn out onto floured board, cover with plastic wrap, then a towel, and allow to rest 20 minutes. Punch down dough and shape into 2 loaves. Place in greased 8-inch bread pans. Brush lightly with oil; cover pans lightly with plastic wrap, and refrigerate 2-24 hours. Remove from refrigerator 10 minutes before baking. Preheat oven to 400° F. and bake loaves 30-40 minutes or until they test done.

Note: Recipe can be halved to make 1 loaf, just be certain to use half the amount of flour called for in each of the preliminary beating steps.

WHOLE WHEAT ROLLS   Yield: 2 dozen
A surprisingly light roll — extra nourishing

3¾-4 cups whole wheat flour
2 packages active dry yeast
½ teaspoon baking soda
1½ cups cream-style cottage cheese
½ cup water

¼ cup packed brown sugar
2 tablespoons butter or margarine
2 teaspoons salt
2 eggs

Insert dough hooks. At low speed, thouroughly stir together 1½ cups of the flour, the yeast and soda. Heat together cheese, water, sugar, butter or margarine, and salt just till warm (115 to 120° F.), stirring constantly to melt butter. Add to dry mixture; add eggs. Beat at low speed for 1 minute, scraping bowl constantly. Beat 3 minutes at high speed. At low speed, add enough remaining flour to make a moderately stiff dough. Knead until smooth, about 5 minutes. Total mixing/ kneading time should be 6-8 minutes. Grease a large bowl. Put the ball of dough in the bowl and roll the ball to grease the dough. Cover; let rise until nearly doubled. Punch down. Shape into 24 rolls. Place in greased muffin pans. Let rise until nearly doubled. Bake in preheated 375° F. oven for 12-15 minutes.

MULTI-PURPOSE BASIC SWEET YEAST DOUGH

½ cup warm water (110° F.)
2 packages active dry yeast
1½ cups scalded milk
½ cup melted butter or margarine

2 eggs
7 cups all-purpose flour
½ cup granulated sugar
2 teaspoons salt

Insert dough hooks into mixer. Dissolve yeast in warm water, and allow to stand 5 minutes. Scald milk and let cool to lukewarm. Combine butter, eggs, and milk and add 2 cups flour, sugar and salt. Knead until blended. Gradually add remaining flour. Dough will form a ball and clean sides of bowl. Total kneading time should be 6-8 minutes. Place in large greased bowl and roll the ball to grease the dough. Cover and let rise until double, about 90 minutes. Punch down, cover and let rise again about 30 minutes. Punch down. Form into rolls desired.

VARIATIONS:

CRESCENT ROLLS

Divide dough into 3 pieces. Roll each piece of dough into a ¼-inch thick circle. Cut into triangles. Beginning at rounded end of triangle, roll dough toward center point. Place on greased cookie sheet. Cover and let rise 20-30 minutes. Bake at 350° F. for 15-20 minutes — until golden brown.

QUICK CLOVERLEAF ROLLS

Form into balls 2-inches in diameter. Place in greased muffin cups. With clean kitchen scissors, snip each ball in half and then in quarters. Cover and let rise 20-30 minutes. Bake at 350° F. for 15-20 minutes — until golden brown.

CLOVERLEAF ROLLS

Form into balls 1-inch in diameter. Place 3 balls into each greased muffin cup. Cover and let rise 20-30 minutes. Bake at 350° F. for 15-20 minutes — until golden brown.

FAN TAILS

Roll dough to ⅛-inch thickness. Spread with melted butter. Cut strips of dough 1½-inches wide. Stack 6 strips evenly. Cut into 1-inch pieces. Place cut end of fan tail down in greased muffin cup. Fill the rest of the muffin cups in the same manner. Cover and let rise 20-30 minutes. Bake at 350° F. for 15-20 minutes — until golden brown.

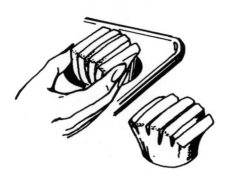

KNOTS

Roll dough to ½-inch thickness. Cut into 1-inch strips, 6-inches long. Tie into knots and press ends down onto greased cookie sheet. Cover and let rise 20-30 minutes. Bake at 350° F. for 15-20 minutes — until golden brown.

FIGURE 8's

Roll dough to ½-inch thickness. Cut into 1-inch strips, 8-inches long. Attach 2 ends together. Twist once to form a figure 8. Place on greased cookie sheet. Cover and let rise 20-30 minutes. Bake at 350° F. for 20-25 minutes — until golden brown.

TWISTS

Use same procedure as "Figure 8's." Give dough an additional twist. Bake as described for "Figure 8's."

SNAILS

Roll dough into ½-inch thickness. Cut into 1-inch strips, 8-inches long. Place an end of dough strip on a greased cookie sheet. Wind dough around and around in a circle. Tuck end under. If desired, use filling. Cover

and let rise 20-30 minutes. Bake at 350° F. for 20-30 minutes — until golden brown.

COFFEE CAKE RING

Use ½ of Multi-purpose sweet dough recipe. Grease a 10-inch tube pan. Roll dough into individual, golf ball-sized balls. Dip each ball into melted margarine. Then dip into a mixture of ½ cup granulated sugar and 2 teaspoons cinnamon. Fill bottom of tube pan with dough balls. Dough balls should be touching each other. Cover and let rise 30-40 minutes. Bake at 325° F. for 30-40 minutes. Top should be golden brown, and sound hollow when tapped with knuckles.

SWEDISH TEA RING

Use ½ of Multi-purpose sweet dough recipe. Roll dough into a rectangle 14-inches long × 10-inches wide. Combine ½ cup granulated sugar and 2 teaspoons cinnamon. Sprinkle sugar mixture over rectangle. Distribute ½ cup raisins; ¼ cup maraschino cherries, coarsely chopped; and ¼ cup chopped nuts over dough. Roll up tightly at wide end. (You should have a long tube-shaped roll.) Seal seam. Form a ring and seal ends together. With a pair of scissors, cut ⅔ of the way through the ring at 1-inch intervals. Turn sections on their side. Cover and let rise 20-30 minutes. Bake at 350° F. for 35-40 minutes. Top should be golden brown, and should sound hollow when tapped with knuckles.

VERONA BREAD
Yield: 3 loaves

An Italian Easter Bread

1 package active dry yeast
1 cup lukewarm water (110-115°F.)
6 tablespoons butter or margarine
½ cup granulated sugar
4 eggs
1 tablespoon grated lemon rind
1 teaspoon vanilla extract

1 teaspoon salt
4¼-5 cups all-purpose flour
6 tablespoons butter or margarine
2 tablespoons granulated sugar
2 tablespoons melted butter or
   margarine
Slivered blanched or sliced almonds

Grease a large bowl and set aside. Dissolve yeast in warm water. In a large mixer bowl, cream together the first 6 tablespoons of butter or margarine and sugar; beat in the eggs individually; add grated lemon rind, vanilla and salt. Add yeast mixture and beat until smooth. Insert dough hooks and add 4¼ cups flour. Stir and knead 6-8 minutes, kneading in enough flour to make a soft, smooth ball of dough. Place in greased bowl and roll the ball to grease the dough. Cover and let rise in a warm place until double in bulk. Punch down.

On a lightly floured board roll out dough to a long rectangle about ½-inch thick. Sliver 2 tablespoons butter across center third of dough, fold first one side over the center third, then the other side. Wrap loosely in waxed paper and refrigerate for 20 minutes. Repeat this rolling, buttering and folding twice, using 2 tablespoons butter each time. After the third chilling, divide dough into 3 pieces and shape each into a round ball. Place in 3 buttered 8-inch pans. Brush with melted butter, sprinkle with sugar, and press almonds into the top. Cover and let rise in a warm place until double, about 1 hour. Preheat oven to 350° F. Bake 35-40 minutes or until bread tests done.

CHALLAH   Yield: 2 loaves

A traditional Jewish Sabbath bread, Challah should be light in texture, and definitely not sweet. Glazed with egg yolk and sprinkled with poppy seeds, it is beautiful to behold.

2 packages active dry yeast
1½ cups warm water
2 tablespoons granulated sugar
1 tablespoon salt
4 tablespoons shortening

3 eggs
5 to 5½ cups all-purpose flour
1 egg yolk mixed with 2 teaspoons
   cold water
Poppy seeds

Insert dough hooks. Dissolve yeast in warm water in large mixer bowl. Add sugar, salt, shortening, eggs and 2 cups flour. Beat at high speed 2 minutes. At low speed, mix in remaining flour and knead enough to make a smooth, elastic dough which cleans the sides of the bowl. Total mixing/kneading time should be 6-8 minutes. Place dough in large greased bowl and roll the ball to grease the dough. Place in warm place to rise until doubled in bulk. Punch down.

Divide dough into 6 equal parts. Roll between your hands or on a lightly floured board to form thick ropes. Braid 3 of the ropes together. Pinch ends to seal. Place on a buttered baking sheet. Braid the other 3 ropes. Cover and allow to rise in a warm place until doubled in bulk. Brush tops of loaves with egg-yolk-water mixture, and sprinkle with poppy seeds. Preheat oven to 400° F. and bake 35-45 minutes or until the loaves sound hollow when tapped with your knuckle.

HOT CROSS BUNS   Yield: 18-24

Originally eaten only on Good Friday, these buns are traditional for the entire Lenten season.

1 package active dry yeast
¼ cup warm water
1 cup milk
½ cup butter or margarine
4 cups all-purpose flour
1 teaspoon salt

½ cup granulated sugar
2 eggs
½ cup raisins
¼ cup chopped citron
Topping

Dissolve yeast in warm water. Heat milk and butter or margarine until butter is melted. Cool to lukewarm. Insert dough hooks. In large mixer bowl combine 1 cup flour, salt and sugar; add dissolved yeast and cooled milk. Beat at high speed 1 minute. Add 1 cup flour and the eggs and beat 2 minutes. Add fruit, then add remaining flour, at low speed, kneading to form a smooth, elastic dough. Total mixing/kneading time will be about 6 minutes. You may have to add more flour to form a smooth ball of dough that cleans the sides of the bowl..

Grease a large bowl. Place ball of dough in bowl and roll the ball to grease the dough. Put in warm place to rise until doubled. Punch down. Divide into 18-24 small rolls. Place 1 inch apart on greased cookie sheet. Let rise until doubled. With a very sharp knife cut across the top of each round. Bake in preheated oven at 400° F. about 20 minutes. When cool, fill in crosses with topping.

TOPPING

1 cup confectioners' sugar
1 tablespoon milk or cream
¼ teaspoon vanilla extract

Combine. If too thick, thin out with a few drops of water.

CHRISTMAS STOLLEN   Yield: 3 loaves

Wrapped and tied with a pretty ribbon, this makes a welcome holiday gift.

1¼ cups milk, scalded
¾ cup granulated sugar
2 teaspoons salt
½ cup butter or margarine
2 envelopes active dry yeast
¼ cup warm water (110-115° F.)
5-5½ cups all-purpose flour
1 teaspoon lemon rind
½ teaspoon ground cardamom seeds
   (optional)

2 eggs, unbeaten
1 cup raisins
½ cup currants
1 cup (8 ounces) chopped mixed
   candied fruits
½ cup (4 ounces) chopped candied
cherries
1 cup chopped blanched almonds
Melted butter
Glaze (optional)

Insert dough hooks in mixer. Combine scalded milk, sugar, salt, and butter or margarine. Let stand until lukewarm. Soften yeast in warm water. Add 3 cups of the flour to the lukewarm milk mixture; beat well. Add lemon rind, spices, eggs, and dissolved yeast. Beat thoroughly at high speed for 2 minutes. Add remaining flour at low speed, making a soft dough, kneading flour as necessary. Total mixing/kneading time should be 8-10 minutes. The dough should become smooth and elastic and clean the sides of the bowl. Grease a large bowl thoroughly with butter or margarine. Put the ball of dough in the bowl and roll the ball to grease the dough. Cover and let rise in warm place until double in bulk — about 1½ hours.

Combine fruits and nuts. When dough is ready, punch down and return to mixer bowl. At low speed, carefully knead in fruit-nut mixture, until evenly distributed. Divide into 3 parts.

Flatten each piece of dough about ¾-inch thick, in the shape of an oval about 12 x 7 inches. Brush lightly with butter. Fold lengthwise about in half so that edges do not quite meet. Press top edge down to seal. Place on greased baking sheets. Brush again with butter and let rise in warm place until double in bulk, 45 minutes. Preheat oven to 350° F. Bake loaves for 25-30 minutes. When cool, spread with glaze. If freezing the loaves, glaze after defrosting. These can be baked in 8-inch loaf pans, if desired, in which case, baking time 45-50 minutes.

GLAZE

Combine 3 cups sifted confectioners' sugar with about 3 tablespoons hot milk. It should be thin enough to spread.

HUNGARIAN COFFEE CAKE

Yield: 12 servings

One recipe Two Loaf Recipe White
  Bread (2 pounds of bread dough)
¼ cup plus 3 tablespoons melted
  butter

1½ cups granulated sugar
2 teaspoons cinnamon
1 cup finely chopped nuts

Grease a 10-inch tube pan. Combine sugar and cinnamon in small bowl. Shape dough into small balls, the size of cherry tomtoes. Roll in melted butter, then in mixture of sugar and cinnamon. Place balls in tube pan. As you fill in a layer, sprinkle with the chopped nuts, sprinkling each layer as you go. Heat oven to 200° F., then turn oven off and place pan of dough balls in oven to allow dough to rise for 1-1½ hours or until they reach top of pan. Remove cake from oven. Preheat oven to 350° F. Bake 20-30 minutes. (Bake even though dark on top.) Let stand to cool in pan for 10 minutes, then invert on plate. Pull off balls to eat. For a gift at holiday time, decorate with red and green candied cherries, wrap in plastic wrap, and tie with a big red bow.

MERINGUE COFFEE CAKE

Yield: 10 servings

1 cup (½ pound) butter or margarine
1½ cups granulated sugar
2 packages active dry yeast
½ cup warm water
3 eggs, separated

1 teaspoon vanilla
4 cups all-purpose flour
½ cup sour cream
Cinnamon
1 cup raisins

Cream margarine or butter with ¼ cup sugar in large mixer bowl. Stir yeast into warm water to dissolve and set aside. Beat egg yolks into creamed mixture; add vanilla. At low speed, alternately add flour, dissolved yeast and sour cream. Mix well. Put in large greased bowl, cover loosely and refrigerate overnight. The next day, roll out the dough to a 12 x 15-inch rectangle. In a large mixer bowl, at high speed, beat egg whites until stiff, beating in remaining 1¼ cups sugar.

Spread this meringue over the dough, sprinkle generously with cinnamon and raisins. Roll up as for jelly roll; pinch edges together firmly to seal. Cut roll into 6 pieces and place cut-side-up in greased 10-inch tube pan. Cover and let rise in warm place for 2 hours; it should rise to the top of the pan. Preheat oven to 350° F. and bake the coffee cake for 55 minutes. The meringue oozes out and forms a topping as the cake bakes.

SOUR CREAM COFFEE CAKE

Yield: 10 servings

¾ cup butter or margarine
1½ cups granulated sugar
3 eggs
1½ cups sour cream
1½ teaspoons vanilla extract

3 cups all-purpose flour
1½ teaspoon baking powder
1½ teaspoon baking soda
¼ teaspoon salt

FILLING:

½ cup brown sugar, packed
¼ cup granulated sugar
1½ teaspoons cinnamon

½ cup finely chopped walnuts
1 cup semi-sweet chocolate bits
(optional)

Grease thoroughly a 10-inch angel food pan, Bundt cake pan, or two 9-inch loaf pans. In a mixer bowl, cream butter and sugar until light and fluffy. Beat in eggs and sour cream until very creamy and light. Add vanilla. Stir in dry ingredients, beating until combined. In a separate small bowl, combine filling ingredients. Pour one third of batter into baking pan, sprinkle on half of filling; add another third of batter and cover with remaining filling. Pour on remaining batter. Bake at 350° F. 1 hour or until done. Allow cake to cool in pan for 20 minutes before inverting onto cooling rack.

VARIATION

CRANBERRY FILLING

You may wish to substitute for a filling, a 1 pound can of whole cranberry sauce. Layer the batter with cranberry sauce. If desired, almond extract can replace half the vanilla in the batter.

COMPANY COFFEE CAKE   Yield: 8 servings

1¼ cups sifted cake flour
2 teaspoons baking powder
½ teaspoon salt
¼ cup butter or margarine
1 cup granulated sugar

2 egg yolks
½ cup milk
2 egg whites, stiffly beaten
¼ teaspoon vanilla extract
Topping

Measure sifted flour, add baking powder and salt and sift again. Grease thoroughly a 9 x 9 x 2-inch pan. Preheat oven to 350° F. Cream butter until fluffy, add sugar and cream at medium speed until very light. Add yolks one at a time, beating thoroughly after each addition. Add dry ingredients alternately with milk, beating smooth at low speed. Fold in the stiffly beaten egg whites; stir in vanilla. Pour batter into prepared pan and bake 30 minutes or until lightly browned and just firm in center. Remove carefully from oven and very quickly sprinkle Topping over cake and return to oven. Bake about 15 minutes longer. Serve warm.

TOPPING:

½ cup all-purpose flour
½ cup granulated sugar
1½ teaspoons cinnamon

¼ teaspoon salt
½ cup firmly packed brown sugar
¼ cup butter

Sift together flour, granulated sugar, cinnamon and salt. Stir in brown sugar. Cut in butter with mixer or with pastry blender, until you have a crumbly mixture.

BISCUITS   Yield: 8 (2-inch)

2 cups all-purpose flour
1 tablespoon baking powder
½ tablespoon salt

¾ cup milk
¼ cup margarine, melted

Preheat oven to 450° F. Insert dough hooks into mixer. Into a large mixing bowl, sift flour, baking powder and salt. Add milk and margarine. Mix ingredients on low speed until blended, approximately 30 seconds. Scrape sides of bowl, as necessary. Place dough on a lightly floured board. Cover with waxed paper. Roll to ½-inch thickness. Cut into rounds with a biscuit cutter. Place on an ungreased baking sheet. Bake for 15-20 minutes.

SCOTTISH CREAM SCONES

Yield: 16 scones

2 cups all-purpose flour, sifted
¾ teaspoon salt
1 teaspoon granulated sugar
1 teaspoon baking powder
1 teaspoon baking soda

1 cup sour cream
5 tablespoons melted butter or
   margarine
1 cup raisins

Insert dough hooks into mixer. Sift flour, salt, sugar, baking powder and baking soda into large mixer bowl. Add sour cream, margarine and raisins. Mix thoroughly on medium-low speed. Divide dough into 4 parts. Pat each part into a circle 1-inch thick. Cut circles into quarters. Cook dough slowly on lightly greased griddle at 300° F. (about 20 minutes). Turn scones frequently for even browning.

POPOVERS

Yield: 8 rolls

Serve piping hot right out of the oven with plenty of butter

2 eggs
1 cup milk
1 tablespoon butter or margarine,
   melted

1 cup sifted all-purpose flour
½ teaspoon salt

Preheat oven to 425° F. Grease thoroughly eight 5-ounce custard cups and arrange on a cookie sheet. If you are fortunate enough to own cast-iron popover pans, heat them in the oven; brush with melted butter just before pouring in the popover batter.

Beat eggs in large mixer bowl. Add milk and butter or margarine; beat until blended. Add flour and salt and continue beating until the batter is smooth. Ladle into custard cups, filling each ½ full. Bake 35 minutes or until deep brown. Serve at once.

GINGER MUFFINS   Yield: 3½ dozen

2 teaspoons baking soda
1 cup buttermilk
4 cups all-purpose flour
½ teaspoon ground cinnamon
½ teaspoon ground allspice
½ teaspoon ground ginger

½ teaspoon salt
1 cup butter or margarine, softened
1 cup granulated sugar
4 eggs
1 cup molasses

Preheat oven to 400° F. Combine baking soda and buttermilk and set aside. Sift together flour, cinnamon, allspice, ginger and salt; set aside. In large mixing bowl cream butter or margarine and sugar on high speed until light and fluffy — about 1 minute. Add eggs one at a time, beating well after each addition. Slowly pour in molasses while continuing to beat. Turn to low speed. Add dry ingredients to creamed mixture alternately with buttermilk, beating well after each addition. Fill greased 2-inch muffin pans ⅔ full. Bake at 400° F. for 20 minutes.

BLUEBERRY MUFFINS SUPREME   Yield: 1 dozen

2 cups unsifted all-purpose flour
2 teaspoons baking powder
½ teaspoon salt
½ cup butter or margarine
1 cup granulated sugar
2 eggs

½ cup milk
2½ cups blueberries, washed and
     thoroughly drained
1 teaspoon vanilla extract
2 teaspoons granulated sugar for tops
     of muffins

Preheat oven to 375° F. Grease muffin tins well, greasing entire top of pan. Sift together flour, baking powder and salt. Set aside. On low speed, cream butter and sugar until fluffy. Beat in eggs, one at a time, beating until light. At low speed, add dry ingredients alternately with milk. By hand, mash ½ cup of the blueberries, and stir them, along with the vanilla, into the batter. Continuing to stir by hand, add remaining whole berries. Pile high in the muffin cups. Sprinkle with sugar. Bake 30 minutes or until done. Cool in the pan about 30 minutes.

ORANGE-SPICE BRAN MUFFINS   Yield: 1 dozen

1½ cups whole bran cereal
1 cup milk
1½ cups all-purpose flour
1 tablespoon baking powder
1 tablespoon pumpkin pie spice
½ teaspoon salt

⅓ cup granulated sugar
¼ cup butter or margarine
1 egg, lightly beaten
⅔ cup raisins
1 tablespoon grated orange peel

In a small bowl, combine bran with milk; let stand 3 minutes. Preheat oven to 400° F. Grease a muffin pan. Sift together flour, baking powder, pumpkin pie spice and salt. Insert dough hooks. Add sugar and butter to flour and cut in butter on low speed until mixture resembles coarse crumbs. To bran mixture add egg, raisins and orange peel. At low speed stir into flour mixture just until blended. Fill muffin cups ¾ full. Bake 25 minutes or until golden brown. Serve piping hot.

SPOONBREAD   Yield: 6-8 servings

1 cup cornmeal
3 cups milk, divided
3 eggs, separated

1¼ teaspoon salt
1¼ teaspoon baking powder
2 tablespoons salad oil

Preheat oven to 325° F. Combine cornmeal and 2 cups milk in saucepan; cook over medium heat, stirring constantly, until consistency of mush. Remove from heat and cool. In small mixing bowl beat egg whites on high speed until very stiff — about 1 minute. Set aside. In large mixing bowl beat egg yolks on medium speed for a few seconds. Add cornmeal mixture, salt, baking powder, oil and 1 cup milk. Continue mixing for a few seconds until all ingredients are thoroughly blended. Scrape sides of bowl as necessarry. Turn to low speed. Fold in stiffly beaten egg whites and mix just until blended — a few seconds. Pour mixture into a greased 2-quart baking dish. Bake at 325° F. for 1 hour.

CORNBREAD   Yield: 8-10 servings

1 cup all-purpose sifted flour
¼ cup granulated sugar
4 teaspoons baking powder
¾ teaspoon salt

1 cup cornmeal
2 eggs
1 cup milk
¼ cup melted butter or margarine

Preheat oven to 425° F. Grease a 9 x 9 x 2-inch baking pan. Sift flour, sugar, baking powder and salt into a large mixing bowl. Add cornmeal, eggs, milk and butter. Mix on low speed until mixture is well blended. Scrape side of bowl as necessary. DO NOT OVERBEAT. Pour batter into prepared baking pan. Bake for 20-25 minutes. Remove from oven. While still warm, cut into pieces and serve.

VARIATION

CORNSTICKS

Prepare batter as directed above. Pour into well-greased cornstick pans and bake for 15-20 minutes in a 425° F. oven. Makes 21 cornsticks.

MEXICAN CORNBREAD   Yield: 6-8 servings

1 cup yellow cornmeal
½ teaspoon salt
½ teaspoon baking soda
⅓ cup melted shortening
1 cup commercial sour cream

1 (8 ounce) can cream-style corn
2 eggs, beaten
¾ cup shredded Cheddar cheese
1-2 finely chopped green chiles
¼ cup Parmesan cheese

Preheat oven to 375° F. Combine cornmeal, salt and soda in small mixing bowl. Mix at medium speed while adding shortening, sour cream, corn and eggs. Beat until ingredients are well mixed, about ½ minute. Spoon half of batter into greased 8 or 9-inch baking dish. Sprinkle with cheeses and chiles; cover with remaining cornbread mixture. Bake at 375° F. for 35-40 minutes or until golden brown.

HUSH PUPPIES Yield: 2 dozen

¾ cup all-purpose flour
2 teaspoons baking powder
1 tablespoon granulated sugar
½ teaspoon salt
1¼ cups cornmeal

1 egg, beaten
¾ cup milk
1 small onion, finely chopped
Shortening for deep frying

Sift dry ingredients into small mixing bowl. Add egg and milk and beat on low speed for a few seconds. Add chopped onion and continue mixing just until ingredients are thoroughly blended. Drop batter by teaspoonfuls into deep hot oil (360° F.), frying only a few at a time. Cook until hush puppies are golden brown. Drain on absorbent paper toweling.

BRAN MOLASSES BROWN BREAD Yield: 2 round loaves

1 cup all-purpose flour, sifted
1 teaspoon baking soda
½ teaspoon salt
½ teaspoon cinnamon
1 cup whole wheat bran
½ cup seedless raisins

2 tablespoons melted butter or
  margarine
½ cup molasses
¼ cup hot water
1 egg

Insert dough hooks into mixer. Sift flour, soda, salt and cinnamon into large mixer bowl. Add cereal, raisins, butter, molasses, hot water and egg. Mix thoroughly on medium speed for about ½ minute. Place mixture into 2 well-greased 1 pound vegetable cans. Fill about ⅔ full. Bake at 350° F. for 45 minutes. Remove from cans and let cool on rack.

CHERRY NUT BREAD   Yield: 1 loaf

2 cups all-purpose flour
1 teaspoon baking soda
½ teaspoon salt
½ cup butter or margarine, softened
¾ cup granulated sugar
2 eggs

1 cup buttermilk
1 tablespoon vanilla extract
1 cup chopped walnuts
¾ cup maraschino cherries, drained
　　and chopped

Insert dough hooks. Preheat oven to 350° F. Grease a 9 x 5x 3-inch loaf pan. On a piece of waxed paper, sift flour, baking soda and salt. In a large mixing bowl, cream butter and sugar on high speed for 1 minute. Add eggs and continue mixing until well blended, scraping sides of bowl as necessary. Turn to low speed and alternately add flour mixture and buttermilk and continue mixing until well blended. Scrape sides of the bowl as necessary. Add vanilla, walnuts and maraschino cherries. Mix until thoroughly combined. Pour batter into prepared loaf pan. Bake for 60-70 minutes. Allow to cool in pan for 10 minutes. Remove from pan and place on wire rack. Serve warm or cool.

BANANA NUT BREAD   Yield: 1 (9 x 5 x 3-inch) loaf

2 cups all-purpose flour
½ teaspoon salt
½ teaspoon baking soda
1 cup brown sugar, firmly packed
½ cup butter or margarine, melted

2 eggs
⅓ cup buttermilk
2 large ripe bananas, mashed
½ cup chopped walnuts

Grease and dust with flour a 9 x 5 x 3-inch loaf pan. Insert dough hooks into mixer. Into a large mixing bowl, sift flour, salt and baking soda. Add brown sugar, butter, eggs, buttermilk, bananas and walnuts. Mix thoroughly on medium speed scraping sides of bowl, as necessary. Pour into prepared pan. Let stand 20 minutes. Preheat oven to 350° F. Bake for 80 minutes or until toothpick inserted into the center of bread comes out clean. Remove from pan and cool on wire rack.

IRISH BREAD Yield: 1 (9-inch) loaf

1 cup raisins
1½ cups all-purpose flour
1½ teaspoons baking powder
½ teaspoon salt
½ cup granulated sugar

2 tablespoons shortening
¾ cup milk
1 egg
3 teaspoons caraway seeds

Preheat oven to 350° F. Grease and flour one 9-inch loaf pan. Cover raisins with water and bring to boil; boil for 3 minutes. Drain and dust with a little of the flour. Sift together the remaining flour, baking powder, salt and sugar. Insert dough hooks. Add shortening and cut in at low speed until flour mixture resembles cornmeal. Add milk, egg, caraway seeds, raisins, and stir at low speed to combine. Do not beat. Pour into prepared pan. Bake in preheated oven for 1 hour or until bread tests done.

CRANBERRY-ORANGE BREAD Yield: 1 (9-inch) loaf

1 medium orange
Boiling water
1 egg
2 cups (½ pound) cranberries,
    coarsely chopped
1 cup granulated sugar

¼ cup shortening, melted
2 cups sifted all-purpose flour
1½ teaspoons baking powder
½ teaspoon salt
½ teaspoon baking soda
¾ cup chopped walnuts

Grease a 9 x 5 x 3-inch loaf pan. Cut orange into 8-10 pieces and remove seeds. Using the finest blade of the food chopper attachment, grind the entire orange and put into a measuring cup. Add hot water to make 1 cup. Using small bowl, beat egg thoroughly; add cranberries, sugar, melted shortening and orange mixture. Stir and set aside.

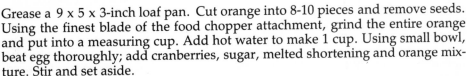

Insert dough hooks. Into large mixer bowl sift flour, baking powder, salt and baking soda. Pour in cranberry-orange mixture and stir together on low speed until thoroughly combined. Scrape sides of bowl often. Do not overbeat. Turn off mixer and by hand fold in walnuts. Pour into prepared pan and allow to stand 15 minutes. In the meantime, preheat oven to 350° F. Bake 55-60 minutes or until done.

APPLESAUCE 'N' OATMEAL LOAF   Yield: 1 (9 x 5 x 3-inch) loaf

1½ cups sifted all-purpose flour
1 teaspoon baking powder
1 teaspoon baking soda
½ teaspoon salt
1 teaspoon cinnamon
½ teaspoon nutmeg
⅔ cup brown sugar, firmly packed

2 eggs
⅓ cup butter or margarine, melted
1 cup raisins
¾ cup chopped walnuts
1½ cups rolled oats
1 cup applesauce

Preheat oven to 350° F. Grease and dust with flour a 9 x 5 x 3-inch loaf pan. Insert dough hooks into mixer. Sift flour, baking powder, baking soda, salt, cinnamon and nutmeg into large mixing bowl. Add brown sugar, eggs, butter, raisins, walnuts, oats and applesauce. Mix thoroughly on medium speed until combined, approximately 30-45 seconds. Pour into prepared loaf pan. Bake for 60 minutes or until a toothpick inserted into center of bread comes out clean. Remove from pan and let cool on wire rack.

APRICOT NUT BREAD   Yield: 1 loaf

2 cups all-purpose flour
2 teaspoons baking powder
¼ teaspoon baking soda
¾ teaspoon salt
1 cup granulated sugar
½ cup water

¼ cup orange juice
1 egg
2 tablespoons butter or margarine
1 cup chopped nutmeats
½ cup dried apricots, chopped

Insert dough hooks into mixer. Sift flour, baking powder, baking soda and salt into large mixer bowl. Add sugar, water, juice, egg, butter, nuts and apricots. Mix thoroughly on medium speed — about 1 minute. Pour into a greased and floured 9 x 5 x 3-inch pan. Bake at 350° F. for 60 minutes or until toothpick inserted in center comes out clean. Remove from pan and let cool on rack.

PUMPKIN BREAD

Yield: 1 loaf

1¾ cup all-purpose flour
½ teaspoon baking powder
1 teaspoon salt
1 teaspoon baking soda
¼ teaspoon ground cloves
¾ teaspoon ground cinnamon
½ teaspoon ground nutmeg

¾ teaspoon ground allspice
1 cup granulated sugar
½ cup salad oil
2 eggs, beaten
1 cup cooked, mashed pumpkin
¼ cup water

Preheat oven to 350° F. Sift together flour, baking powder, salt, soda, cloves, cinnamon, nutmeg and allspice and set aside. Combine sugar, oil and eggs in large mixing bowl and beat on high speed until light and fluffy or about 1 minute. Turn to low speed. Gradually add pumpkin and dry ingredients alternately with water and continue mixing for about 1 minute or until thoroughly blended.

Spoon batter into a well-greased 9 x 5 x 3-inch loaf pan. Bake at 350° F. for 65-70 minutes. **Suggested toppings:** Cream Cheese Frosting or Whipped Cream Cheese.

DATE NUT LOAF

Yield: 1 loaf

1 cup boiling water
½ teaspoon baking soda
1½ cups chopped dates
1¼ cups all-purpose flour, sifted
2 teaspoons baking powder
¾ teaspoon salt

¾ cup brown sugar, packed
1 egg
2 tablespoons melted butter or
  margarine
½ cup chopped pecans or walnuts

Insert dough hooks into mixer. Combine water, baking soda and dates and let cool. In large mixer bowl combine flour, baking powder and salt. On medium speed blend cooled date mixture with dry ingredients. Add brown sugar, egg, margarine and nuts. Mix just until blended (20-30 seconds). Pour into greased and floured 9 x 5 x 3-inch pan. Bake at 350° F. for 75 minutes or until toothpick inserted in center comes out clean. Remove from pan and let cool.

ZUCCHINI BREAD   Yield: 2 loaves

3¼ cups all-purpose flour
1 teaspoon baking powder
1 teaspoon baking soda
1 tablespoon cinnamon
1 teaspoon salt
2 cups zucchini, grated and drained

3 eggs
1 cup salad oil
1 cup granulated sugar
1 cup raisins
1 cup chopped nuts

Preheat oven to 350° F. Sift together dry ingredients. Grease thoroughly two 8-inch loaf pans. Using finest disc on grinder, grate the zucchini. Beat eggs thoroughly in large mixer bowl. Beat in the oil and sugar, beating till creamy. Add zucchini on low speed, add the sifted dry ingredients. By hand, stir in raisins and nuts. Bake 1 hour in greased and floured 9 x 5 x 3-inch pans. Cool in pans for 15 minutes before inverting onto cooling racks. Wrapped airtight, this bread keeps well in the refrigerator. It also freezes well.

Chapter Two
CAKES AND FROSTINGS

BASIC YELLOW CAKE   Yield: 2 layers

2 cups sifted cake flour
1¼ cups granulated sugar
2½ teaspoons double-acting
  baking powder
¾ teaspoon salt

½ cup soft shortening
¾ cup milk
1¼ teaspoons vanilla extract
2 eggs

Preheat oven at 375° F. Grease and dust with flour, two 8-inch layer pans. In large mixing bowl sift flour, sugar, baking powder and salt. Add shortening, pour in ½ cup milk and vanilla. Beat ½ minute on low speed to moisten flour mixture; beat ½ minute on medium speed, scraping sides of bowl as necessary. Add eggs and remaining ¼ cup milk. Beat ½ minute on medium speed. Divide batter evenly into pans. Bake 25-30 minutes at 375° F. Cake is done when toothpick inserted in center comes out clean. Remove pans from oven, invert each layer onto a cake cooling rack, remove pans and cool to room temperature before frosting.

Suggested topping: Butter Cream, Maple Cream, Chocolate Cream Frosting.

BASIC WHITE CAKE   Yield: 2 layers

2½ cups sifted cake flour
1½ cups granulated sugar
3 teaspoons double-acting
  baking powder
1 teaspoon salt

½ cup shortening
1 cup milk
1½ teaspoons vanilla extract
¼ teaspoon almond extract
3 egg whites

Set oven at 350 ° F. to preheat. Grease and dust with flour, two 8-inch layer pans. Sift flour, sugar, baking powder and salt into a large mixing bowl. Add shortening, ¾ cup milk and flavorings. Beat on low speed just long enough to moisten flour, then on medium speed for 1 minute, scraping bowl as necessary. Add remaining ¼ cup milk and egg whites, beat ½ minute longer. Divide evenly into prepared pans. Bake about 30 minutes at 350° F. Cake is done when toothpick inserted in center comes out clean. Remove pans from oven, invert each layer onto a cake cooling rack, remove pans, and cool to room temperature before frosting.

Suggested Topping: Butter Cream Frosting, Chocolate Cream Frosting, Maple Cream Frosting.

COCOA DEVIL'S FOOD CAKE

Yield: 2 layers

1½ cups sifted cake flour
1¼ cups granulated sugar
½ cup cocoa
¾ teaspoon salt
1¼ teaspoon baking soda

⅔ cup soft shortening
1 cup buttermilk
1 teaspoon vanilla extract
2 eggs

Preheat oven to 350° F. Grease and dust with flour two 8-inch round cake pans. Sift together flour, sugar, cocoa, salt, baking soda in large mixing bowl. Add shortening, ⅔ cup buttermilk and vanilla. Combine ingredients on low speed for 2 minutes, scraping sides of bowl as necessary. Add 2 eggs and remaining ⅓ cup buttermilk and stir on low speed for 2 minutes. Pour in prepared pans. Bake at 350° F. for 30-35 minutes. Remove from pans and cool on rack.

CHOCOLATE NUT TORTE

Yield: 3 cake layers

3 squares unsweetened chocolate
2 cups unsifted cake flour
1 teaspoon baking soda
1 teaspoon salt
⅓ cup softened butter or margarine

1 cup sour cream
1½ cups granulated sugar
2 eggs
1 teaspoon almond extract
1 cup hot water (110-120° F.)

Preheat oven to 350° F. Grease and dust with flour three 8-inch cake pans. Melt chocolate in double boiler. Cool. On a piece of waxed paper, sift flour, baking soda and salt. In a large mixing bowl, combine butter, sour cream and sugar. Cream on medium speed for 2 minutes. Scrape sides of bowl as necessary. Add eggs, almond extract and chocolate, and continue mixing until well blended, about 2 minutes. Turn to low speed and add flour mixture and water. After dry ingredients are moistened, turn to medium speed and mix for 2 minutes. Scrape sides of bowl as necessary. Divide the batter into 3 parts, and pour into prepared cake pans. Bake for 30-35 minutes or until a toothpick inserted into center comes out clean. Cool cake in pans for 5 minutes. Loosen edges of cake with a spatula and turn onto wire racks. Cool completely before frosting.

Suggested Topping:

NUT FILLING

¾ cup granulated sugar
¾ cup evaporated milk
3 egg yolks
½ cup butter or margarine

1 teaspoon vanilla extract
1½ cups (3½ ounces) flaked coconut
1 cup chopped walnuts

Combine sugar, evaporated milk, egg yolks, butter and vanilla extract in saucepan. Cook over medium heat, stirring constantly until thickened. Remove from heat. Stir in coconut and walnuts. Cool. Spread onto cake layers. Cover cake and chill before serving.

AUTHENTIC POUND CAKE   Yield: 2 loaves

1 pound butter, softened
1 pound granulated sugar (2¼ cups)
1 pound sifted all-purpose flour
  (4 cups)
9 eggs

1 tablespoon lemon juice
1 tablespoon grated lemon rind
  (optional)

Preheat oven to 350° F. Grease two 9 x 5 x 3-inch loaf pans. Add butter to large mixing bowl. Cream on medium speed. Gradually add sugar and continue beating until mixture is light and fluffy, approximately 6-7 minutes. Scrape sides of bowl, as necessary. Turn to low speed. Add eggs, one at a time, beating well after each addition. Turn mixer to medium-low; gradually add flour, lemon juice and rind. Beat until thoroughly blended, scraping sides of bowl as necessary. Pour batter into prepared pans. Bake for 1 hour 15 minutes or until toothpick inserted into center of cake comes out clean. Cool cake in pans for 10 minutes, then invert onto wire racks. Cool to room temperature.

ANGEL FOOD CAKE   Yield: 8-10 servings

1⅔ cups egg whites
  (approximately a dozen)
1 cup plus 2 tablespoons sifted cake
  flour, divided
1¾ cups granulated sugar, divided

1½ teaspoons cream of tartar
½ teaspoon salt
1 teaspoon vanilla extract
1 teaspoon almond extract

Allow egg whites to set at room temperature for 1 hour before mixing. Preheat oven to 375° F. Sift four times onto a sheet of waxed paper, the cake flour and ¾ cup sugar. In a large mixing bowl, combine egg whites, cream of tartar, salt, vanilla extract and almond extract. Beat on high speed, until egg whites form soft peaks. DO NOT OVERBEAT. Turn to medium speed and rapidly sprinkle in remaining 1 cup of sugar. Scrape sides of bowl, as necessary. Turn to lowest speed, and gradually add sifted flour mixture. When all of the flour mixture has been added, stop mixer. Using a rubber spatula, cut through batter several times, folding over and over. Spoon batter into an ungreased 10 x 4-inch tube pan. Push batter to edges of pan all around. Bake for 30-35 minutes, or until toothpick inserted into center of cake comes out clean. Immediately, invert on a funnel or bottle neck and allow to cool completely. Then carefully run a clean spatula around the edges of the pan. Loosen around tube, invert onto cake plate, loosen bottom, and lift off.

Suggested Topping: Vanilla glaze, fresh strawberries.

BANANA CAKE   Yield: 2 layers

2¼ cups cake flour
2½ teaspoons baking powder
½ teaspoon baking soda
½ teaspoon salt
½ cup shortening

1¼ cups granulated sugar
2 eggs
1½ cups mashed ripe bananas
1½ teaspoons vanilla extract

Preheat oven to 375° F. Grease and dust with flour two 8-inch cake pans. Onto a piece of waxed paper, sift cake flour, baking powder, baking soda and salt. In a large mixing bowl, cream shortening and sugar on high speed for 1 minute. Add eggs, bananas and vanilla and continue beating for 1 more minute. Turn to low speed and add cake flour, baking powder, baking soda and salt. When ingredients are moistened, turn to medium speed and beat until mixture is well blended. Pour into prepared cake pans. Bake for 30 minutes or until toothpick inserted in center comes out clean. Remove cake from pans and cool on wire racks before frosting.

Suggested Frosting: Chocolate fudge frosting, Fluffy butter frosting, Quick egg white frosting.

TAFFY'S FRUITCAKE   Yield: 6-8 servings

A marble poundcake rich with fruit.

2 cups all-purpose flour
¼ teaspoon baking soda
¼ teaspoon salt
1 cup butter or margarine
1 cup granulated sugar
4 eggs
⅓ cup citron
⅓ cup candied cherries

⅓ cup candied pineapple
1 teaspoon lemon extract
2 tablespoons unsweetened cocoa
2 tablespoons strong coffee, cooled
1 cup raisins
1 cup walnuts
1 teaspoon vanilla extract
⅓ cup corn syrup

Preheat oven 325° F. Grease thoroughly one 9-inch loaf pan or an 8-inch deep casserole dish. Sift together the flour, baking soda and salt. With electric mixer at medium speed cream butter and sugar until light and fluffy. Add eggs one at a time, beating well after each addition. Stir in dry ingredients. Divide batter in half, putting one half into a small bowl.

To one half of the batter add the candied fruits and lemon extract. To the other half add remaining ingredients. Spoon mixtures into pan, alternating a tablespoon of light and dark batter. Cover pan tightly with aluminum foil and bake 60-75 minutes, or until toothpick inserted in center comes out clean. Cool in pan, covered. Do not uncover until ready to serve. This cake should be overwrapped with plastic wrap and allowed to mellow a few days. When ready to serve, heat ⅓ cup of light corn syrup and drizzle over top of cake. Cut up a few cherries and pieces of citron to make flowers to decorate the top.

LIL'S LIGHT FRUIT CAKE   Yield: 2 loaves

3½ cups all-purpose flour
2 teaspoons baking powder
Dash salt
2 cups granulated sugar
1 cup raisins
½ cup currants or yellow raisins

1 cup chopped walnuts
1 cup shortening
3 eggs
1 teaspoon vanilla extract
1 cup milk

Preheat oven to 350° F. Grease and flour two 8-inch loaf pans. Sift together the dry ingredients, reserving 2 tablespoons flour. Toss the 2 tablespoons flour with the raisins or currants and walnuts in another bowl. In medium bowl of mixer cream the sugar and shortening at medium speed until light; beat in eggs one at a time and add vanilla. At low speed, stir in dry ingredients alternately with milk. Turn mixer off and stir in fruits and nuts by hand. Pour into prepared pans and bake for 15 minutes at 350° F.; then turn oven down to 325° F. and bake 1 hour or until done. Cool in pans 10 minutes, then cool on racks.

CRANBERRY ORANGE CAKE   Yield: 10-12 servings

1½ cups cranberry orange relish
1 package yellow cake mix
½ cup (3 ounces) orange gelatin

¼ cup water
¼ cup salad oil
4 eggs

Preheat oven to 350° F. Grease and flour a 13 x 9 x 2-inch pan. Reserve ¼ cup relish for frosting. Combine cake mix, gelatin, water, oil and eggs and 1¼ cup relish. Using your electric mixer, beat as recommended on the package. Bake 35-40 minutes.

FROSTING: Use Fluffy White Frosting and stir in the reserved Cranberry Orange Relish.

PEACH TRIFLE Yield: 12 servings

CAKES

1 cup sifted cake flour	2 tablespoons butter or margarine
1 teaspoon baking powder	2 eggs
¼ teaspoon salt	1 cup granulated sugar
½ cup milk	1 teaspoon vanilla extract

Preheat oven to 350° F. Grease and flour two 8-inch round cake pans. Sift together flour, baking powder and salt. In small saucepan, heat milk and butter or margarine until melted; keep hot. Beat eggs on high speed until thick and lemon-colored, 3-5 minutes. Gradually add sugar, beating at medium speed for 4-5 minutes. Add sifted dry ingredients and stir slowly just to blend. Stir in hot milk mixture at low speed, add vanilla; blend well. Turn into cake pans and bake 20 minutes or until cakes test done. Cool in pans 10 minutes; remove from pans and cool on rack.

PUDDING

⅓ cup granulated sugar	4 cups sliced peaches (about 5-6
1 tablespoon cornstarch	peaches), peeled
⅛ teaspoon salt	1 tablespoon lemon juice
1 cup milk	¼ cup granulated sugar
2 beaten egg yolks	⅓ cup orange or apricot liqueur
1 tablespoon butter or margarine	Confectioners' sugar
1 teaspoon vanilla extract	Whipped cream
½ cup whipping cream	

Combine sugar, cornstarch and salt in a saucepan. Stir in milk; cook and stir over medium heat until thick and bubbly. Stir a small amount of the hot mixture into beaten egg yolks. Return mixture of milk and egg to pan, stirring constantly. Cool and stir 2 more minutes. Add butter and vanilla; cover surface of pudding with waxed paper or plastic wrap. Refrigerate. Whip ½ cup cream and fold into the chilled pudding. Top sliced peaches with lemon juice. Crush 3½ cups of the fruit and add ¼ cup sugar. Save 12-14 nice slices of peach for top garnish.

TO ASSEMBLE

Split cake layers in half to make 4 layers. Fit a layer into bottom of 1½-quart soufflé dish; spread with ½ the crushed peaches. Top with second cake layer; sprinkle half the liqueur over this layer. Spread with all of the pudding. Place third cake layer on top; spread with remaining peaches. Sprinkle cut side of fourth cake layer with remaining liqueur; place cut side down on top of peaches. Cover with plastic wrap and refrigerate overnight.

To serve, sift confectioners' sugar over the top. Garnish with whipped cream rosettes and reserved sliced peaches.

CARROT CAKE   Yield: 8-10 servings

3 cups all-purpose flour
2 teaspoons baking powder
2 teaspoons baking soda
1 teaspoon salt
2 teaspoons cinnamon
2 cups granulated sugar

1½ cups vegetable oil
4 eggs, unbeaten
3 cups shredded carrots (4-6 whole)
1 cup raisins
½ cup chopped walnuts

Attach the mixer shredder attachment, and shred carrots with fine blade to equal 3 cups. Set aside. Grease and flour a 10-inch tube pan. Preheat oven to 350° F. Sift together flour, baking powder, baking soda, salt and cinnamon. At high speed, beat together sugar and oil until very creamy; add eggs one at a time and beat well. At low speed, stir in carrots, then flour mixture. Lastly, fold in raisins and nuts. Pour into prepared pan and bake 1 hour or until cake tests done. This cake is delicious plain, or with confectioners' sugar sifted over it. If desired, frost with Cream Cheese Frosting.

COCONUT BIRTHDAY CAKE   Yield: 3 layers

2¾ cups sifted cake flour
1¾ cups granulated sugar
2 teaspoons baking powder
1½ teaspoons salt
1 cup vegetable shortening
¾ cup milk

1 teaspoon almond extract
1 teaspoon vanilla extract
3 eggs
1 egg yolk
1 cup shredded coconut,
    finely chopped

Preheat oven to 375° F. Grease and flour three 9-inch layer pans. Combine cake flour with sugar, baking powder and salt, and sift into mixing bowl. Add shortening, milk, flavoring and one of the eggs. Beat at low speed 2 minutes. Scrape bowl and beaters, and add 2 remaining eggs and the yolk and beat again for 2 minutes. At low speed, stir in finely chopped coconut. Pour batter into prepared pans. Bake until done, about 25 minutes. Cool in pans 15 minutes before removing layers to a cooling rack to cool thoroughly. Put layers together and frost with Rum Butter Frosting. Cover top and sides of cake with more shredded coconut.

RAISIN-ORANGE CAKE   Yield: 8-10 servings

1 large orange, juiced
  (reserve juice for frosting)
1 cup seedless raisins
⅓ cup walnuts
2 cups sifted all-purpose flour
1 teaspoon baking soda

1 teaspoon salt
1 cup granulated sugar
½ cup vegetable shortening
¾ cup milk
2 eggs
¼ cup milk

Preheat oven to 350° F. Grease and flour a 9 x 13 x 2-inch pan or two 8 or 9-inch layer pans. Using the coarse blade of the grinder attachment, first grind the entire orange, then the raisins, then walnuts. Reserve. Sift together into large mixer bowl the flour, baking soda, salt and sugar. Add the shortening and ¾ cup milk. At low speed, stir to blend, then beat at medium speed for 2 minutes, scraping bowl often. Add eggs and remaining milk and beat for 2 more minutes. Turn mixer to low speed and fold in the raisin-orange mixture. Pour the batter into prepared pans and bake in preheated oven 35-45 minutes for layers, 40-50 minutes for sheet.

Suggested frosting: Orange Butter

MISSISSIPPI MUD   Yield: 24 servings

1½ cups all-purpose flour
½ teaspoon baking soda
¼ teaspoon baking powder
½ teaspoon salt
⅓ cup unsweetened cocoa
1 cup (½ pound) very soft butter or
  margarine

2 cups granulated sugar
4 eggs
1 teaspoon vanilla extract
2 cups shredded coconut
1½ cups chopped pecans
1 (7 ounce) jar marshmallow creme

Preheat oven to 350° F. Grease thoroughly a 13 x 9 x 2-inch pan. Sift together flour, baking soda, baking powder, salt and cocoa. At medium speed, cream butter and sugar. At very low speed, stir in eggs, one at a time; add vanilla and sifted dry ingredients. Turn mixer off and stir in by hand the coconut and pecans. Pour into prepared pan and bake 30-35 minutes. As soon as you remove it from the oven spread with the marshmallow creme and allow to cool completely. Frost with the following:

CHOCOLATE FROSTING

½ cup butter or margarine, softened
1 (1 pound) box confectioners' sugar
⅓ cup unsweetened cocoa

⅛ teaspoon salt
⅓ cup milk
1 teaspoon vanilla extract

Cream butter; add part of the sugar, then remaining ingredients. Beat till smooth; beat in remaining sugar. If desired, 1 cup of finely chopped pecans can be added to the topping.

ORANGE NUT CAKE

Yield: 1 (9 x 9 x 2-inch) cake layer

3 eggs
1 cup granulated sugar
2 cups graham cracker crumbs
1 teaspoon baking powder
¼ teaspoon salt
1 teaspoon vanilla extract

1 (6 ounce) can frozen orange juice
  concentrate
¾ cup chopped nuts
1 (8 ounce) package pitted dates,
  chopped
Confectioners' sugar

Preheat oven to 350° F. Grease and dust with flour a 9 x 9 x 2-inch pan. Beat eggs in a large mixing bowl on high speed until light and fluffy, about 1 minute. Turn to low speed. Add sugar, graham cracker crumbs, baking powder, salt, vanilla extract and orange juice concentrate. When dry ingredients are moistened, turn to medium speed and mix for 1-2 minutes, or until well blended. Turn mixer to OFF. Stir in nuts and dates. Pour into prepared pan and bake for 45-50 minutes. Remove from oven and cool in pan. When cool, dust lightly with confectioners' sugar.

APPLESAUCE-RAISIN CAKE

Yield: 1 10-inch Bundt cake

1½ cups raisins
½ cup butter or margarine
1 egg
1 cup water
2 cups all-purpose flour
2 teaspoons cinnamon
1 teaspoon allspice

1 teaspoon cloves
¾ teaspoon salt
1¼ teaspoon baking soda
1 teaspoon baking powder
2 cups granulated sugar
1 (16 ounce) can applesauce
1½ cups chopped pecans

Preheat oven to 350° F. Place raisins, butter or margarine and 1 cup water in small pan. Heat mixture to boiling point. Remove from heat, cover with lid and cool. Sift all dry ingredients together and set aside. Combine sugar and applesauce in large mixing bowl and beat at medium speed for about 1 minute. Add egg, sifted dry ingredients, cooled raisin mixture and nuts. Beat just until all ingredients are combined — about 1 minute. Pour mixture into well-greased 10-inch Bundt pan and bake at 350° F. for 1 hour or until toothpick inserted into center comes out clean. Remove pan from oven, invert onto a cake cooling rack, remove pan and cool to room temperature.

Suggested Topping: Sprinkle with ¼ cup confectioners' sugar.

APRICOT CAKE Yield: 1 (10-inch) Bundt cake

2 cups all-purpose flour
2 cups granulated sugar
2 teaspoons baking soda
½ teaspoon salt
1½ teaspoons cinnamon

4 eggs
1¼ cups cooking oil
¾ cup chopped pecans
1 (7¾ ounce) jar apricot baby food

Preheat oven to 350° F. Sift dry ingredients together and set aside. Place eggs in large mixing bowl and beat on high speed until thickened — about 1 minute. Turn to medium speed. Slowly add oil, sifted dry ingredients and nuts. Add strained apricots and continue beating just until all ingredients are thoroughly blended. Pour into a well-greased 10-inch tube or Bundt pan and bake at 350° F. for 1 hour or until a toothpick inserted into center of cake comes out clean. Remove pan from oven, invert onto a cake cooling rack, remove pan and cool to room temperature.

Suggested Topping: Butter Cream Frosting

SACHER TORTE Yield: 1 (9-inch) torte

A torte is a heavy textured cake. This is a super-rich, super-delicious chocolate cake.

6 eggs, separated
¾ cup butter
¾ cup granulated sugar

6 ounces semisweet chocolate,
  melted and cooled
1 teaspoon vanilla extract
2 cups sifted cake flour

Butter and flour two 9-inch layer pans. Preheat oven to 300° F. Beat egg whites stiff and set aside. Cream butter and sugar until fluffy; beat in cooled chocolate. Beat in egg yolks, one at a time; add vanilla. At low speed fold in cake flour and egg whites. Pour batter into pans and bake about 25 minutes, or until they test done. Turn out on cooling rack. Fill layers with apricot jam and frost with Vienna Chocolate icing.

LINZER TORTE   Yield: 6-8 servings

1½ cups sifted all-purpose flour
¼ teaspoon salt
1 cup sifted granulated sugar
1 cup butter
3 egg yolks
Grated rind of one lemon

1 cup unblanched almonds,
  pulverized in a blender
½ teaspoon cinnamon
¼ teaspoon cloves
Raspberry jam

Sift flour and salt. Cream together sugar and butter until very light and fluffy. Beat in the egg yolks, one at a time, and the lemon rind. At low speed, gradually stir in dry ingredients alternately with pulverized almonds, combined with cinnamon and cloves.

Preheat oven to 375° F. Roll out half of the dough to make a circle ½-inch thick to cover the bottom of a springform pan or flat ring. Make side ¼-inch thick and about 1½-inches high. Spread the dough with raspberry jam. Roll out remaining dough and cut into strips. Make a lattice over the jam. Bake 40-50 minutes or until lightly browned. Cool on wire rack. Remove from pan. Fill spaces on top with more jam, dust with confectioners' sugar.

CZECHOSLOVAKIAN CHERRY CAKE   Yield: 8-10 servings

Bublanina

8 ounces fresh cherries
3 eggs
1 cup sifted all-purpose flour
½ teaspoon baking powder
¼ teaspoon salt

½ cup butter or margarine, melted
  and cooled
½ cup granulated sugar
Grated rind of one lemon
½ teaspoon vanilla extract

Wash cherries and dry thoroughly; pit them and set aside.

Separate eggs and allow to stand until they reach room temperature. Melt butter or margarine and set aside to cool. Sift together flour, baking powder and salt. Grease and flour one 9-inch round baking pan. Preheat oven to 350° F.

In small mixer bowl, beat egg whites until soft peaks form; gradually add ¼ cup of the sugar, beating until stiff peaks form. Set aside; beat egg yolks at high speed until thick and lemon-colored, beating in remaining ¼ cup sugar and the grated lemon rind. Turn mixer to low speed and stir in melted butter or margarine and vanilla. Sift the dry ingredients over this, and fold in thoroughly, using lowest mixer speed. Turn mixer off. By hand, fold in thoroughly the stiffly beaten egg whites. Pour this stiff batter into prepared pan and smooth out to sides. Place cherries on top of cake. Bake in preheated oven 35-40 minutes.

Note: Authentically this cake is made with only fresh cherries. However, when unavailable, you can substitute 4 ounces candied cherries. Equally good, you can substitute fresh fruit in season: Blueberries, sliced, pared peaches, nectarines or apples.

GINGERBREAD   Yield: 8-10 servings

2½ cups all-purpose flour
1½ teaspoons baking soda
½ teaspoon salt
1 teaspoon cinnamon
1 teaspoon ground ginger
1 teaspoon ground cloves

½ cup granulated sugar
½ cup butter or margarine
1 egg
1 cup molasses
1 cup hot water

Preheat oven to 350° F. Grease 9 x 9 x 2-inch pan. In small mixing bowl, sift flour, soda, salt, cinnamon, ginger and cloves. Set aside. In large mixing bowl, cream sugar and margarine on high speed for 1 minute. Add egg and molasses and beat for ½ minute. Add hot water and continue beating just until thoroughly mixed. Pour batter into prepared pan. Bake at 350° F. for 35-40 minutes. Cake is done when toothpick inserted in center comes out clean. Serve warm.

Suggested topping: Whipped Cream, Lemon Sauce, Whipped Cream Cheese

PINEAPPLE UPSIDE-DOWN CAKE   Yield: 6-8 servings

3-4 tablespoons butter or margarine
½ cup firmly packed brown sugar
1 small (7½ ounces) can pineapple
    slices, drained

4 maraschino cherries
⅓ cup chopped nuts
1 box (9 ounces) 1-layer yellow
    cake mix

Preheat oven to 350° F. Melt butter or margarine in bottom of 8 x 8 x 2-inch baking pan. Sprinkle with brown sugar and arrange pineapple slices over the sugar. Place cherries in pineapple rings and sprinkle with nuts. In a large mixing bowl, prepare cake mix according to package directions. Scrape sides of bowl as necessary. Pour batter over fruit. Bake for 40-50 minutes or until toothpick inserted into center of cake comes out clean. Invert cake onto serving dish. May be served warm or cool.

Suggested Topping: Whipped Cream Topping

AMARETTO DI SARONNO CAKE   Yield: 8-10 servings

4 eggs
1 box, (1 pound, 2 ounces) orange
   cake mix
1 box (3 ounces) lemon-flavored
   instant pudding mix

2 tablespoons Amaretto di Saronno
   liqueur
½ cup, plus 2 tablespoons water
½ cup butter-flavored oil

Preheat oven to 350° F. Grease a 10-inch Bundt pan. In a large mixing bowl, add eggs and beat on high speed until light, about 1-2 minutes. Turn to low speed and add cake mix, pudding mix, Amaretto di Saronno liqueur, water and oil. When ingredients are moistened, turn to medium speed and beat for 1-2 minutes. Scrape sides of bowl as necessary. Pour batter into prepared Bundt pan. Bake for 35-40 minutes or until toothpick inserted into center of cake comes out clean. Cool in pan. Loosen around sides and tube with a spatula and invert onto a cake plate.

Suggested topping: Amaretto Glaze

GRAHAM CRACKER CAKE   Yield: 2 layers, 8-10 servings

1 box (1 pound, 2 ounces) white
   cake mix
1¼ cups graham cracker crumbs
2 tablespoons granulated sugar

1½ cups water
2 egg whites
¾ cup chopped pecans

Preheat oven to 350° F. Grease and dust with flour two 8-inch round cake pans. In large mixing bowl, combine cake mix, graham cracker crumbs, sugar, water and egg whites. Blend on low speed to moisten ingredients. Turn to medium speed and beat for 3 minutes. Add pecans and mix until evenly distributed. Pour batter into prepared cake pans. Bake for 35-40 minutes or until toothpick inserted in center of cake comes out clean. Cool cake in pans for 5 minutes. Loosen edges of cake with a spatula and turn onto wire racks. Cool completely before frosting.

Suggested frostings: Fluffy butter frosting, Quick egg white frosting, Whipped Cream frosting

STRAWBERRY TORTE Yield: 8-10 servings

A gorgeous cake. Try it for special occasions.

1 cup butter or margarine
1 cup granulated sugar
6 egg yolks
2 cups sifted cake flour
½ teaspoon baking powder
½ teaspoon salt
6 egg whites

¾ cup granulated sugar
3 cups whipping cream
1 tablespoon granulated sugar
1 teaspoon vanilla extract
½ cup currant jelly
1 cup coarsely chopped pecans
1 (12 ounce) jar strawberry preserves

Grease bottoms of three 9-inch layer pans. Preheat oven to 350° F. In large mixer bowl, cream shortening and sugar until very light and fluffy. Add egg yolks, one at a time, beating well after each addition. Beat until very fluffy and smooth, about 5 minutes. Sift together flour, baking powder and salt. Stir dry ingredients into creamed mixture. Beat egg whites to soft peaks; gradually add the ¾ cup sugar, beating to stiff peaks. Fold into batter. Pour into prepared pans and bake 25-30 minutes. Cool completely.

To assemble: Whip the cream with 1 tablespoon sugar and vanilla. Place one cake layer on plate; spread with currant jelly and 1 cup of the whipped cream (measure out 1 cup from all you have beaten). Sprinkle with 2 tablespoons pecans. Place second layer on cake. Spread with ⅔ cup strawberry preserves and 1 cup whipped cream and coat with remaining ¾ cup pecans. Frost top with remaining whipped cream. Swirl remaining ⅓ cup preserves into cream atop cake.

HARVEY WALLBANGER SPONGE CAKE   Yield: 1 sponge cake

6 egg whites
6 egg yolks
1½ cups sifted cake flour
½ teaspoon salt
1 teaspoon baking powder

1½ cups granulated sugar
½ teaspoon cream of tartar
⅓ cup orange juice
2 tablespoons vodka
2 tablespoons Galliano liqueur

Preheat oven to 375° F. Cake is baked in a 10 x 4-inch tube pan. Separate eggs, let stand at room temperature for 1 hour. Sift cake flour, salt, baking powder and 1 cup sugar together. Place egg whites and cream of tartar in large mixing bowl. Beat on high speed until egg whites hold a soft peak. Gradually add remaining ½ cup of sugar and beat until well blended. Set mixture aside. In small mixing bowl combine egg yolks, orange juice, vodka and Galliano. Mix on medium speed for a few seconds. Add dry ingredients and beat until well blended — about ½ minute. Set mixture aside. In large mixing bowl, pour egg yolk mixture over egg whites and fold in at low speed. Use rubber spatula to scrape sides of bowl and help turn mixture over gently. Push batter into ungreased 10 x 4-inch tube pan. Cut through batter with a spatula going around in widening circles 6 times without lifting spatula. Push batter to touch edge of pan all around. Bake for 30-35 minutes. Cake is done when toothpick inserted in center comes out clean. Invert on funnel or bottle neck at once, let hang until completely cold. Then insert spatula between cake and side of pan, press lightly against pan going around and lifting spatula to loosen cake. Loosen around tube, invert on cake plate, loosen bottom and lift off.

JELLY ROLL   Yield: 1 jelly roll

1 cup sifted cake flour
1 teaspoon baking powder
¼ teaspoon salt
3 eggs
½ teaspoon lemon extract

1 teaspoon vanilla extract
1 cup granulated sugar
⅓ cup hot water (110-120° F.)
1 cup confectioners' sugar, divided
¾ cup jelly or jam

Preheat oven to 375° F. Grease a 15 x 10 x 1-inch jelly roll pan. Line with waxed paper and grease waxed paper. On a separate sheet of waxed paper, sift cake flour, baking powder and salt. Set aside. In a large mixing bowl, beat eggs, lemon extract and vanilla extract on high speed for 1 minute. Gradually add sugar. Continue beating until mixture is light and fluffy, about 1-2 minutes. Scrape sides of bowl as necessary. Turn mixer to low speed, add water and flour mixture. After dry ingredients are moistened, turn to medium speed and mix only until blended, about ½ minute. Pour batter into prepared pan and bake 12-14 minutes. While cake is baking, dust tea towel with ¾ cup confectioners' sugar. Remove cake from oven. Turn cake onto prepared tea towel and remove waxed paper immediately. While still hot, roll cake in towel, starting from narrow end. Place on a wire rack, cover with another tea towel, and cool. Unroll cake and spread with jelly or jam. Roll up cake, pulling towel away from cake as you roll. Trim edges, if desired. Place open end down on serving plate. Sift remaining ¼ cup confectioners' sugar over top. Cover until serving time.

ORANGE CAKE Yield: 2 layers

2 cups sifted all-purpose flour
2 teaspoons baking powder
⅛ teaspoon salt
5 eggs, separated

2 cups granulated sugar
Grated rind and juice of 1 large orange
Water
Orange filling

Preheat oven to 350° F. Grease two 9-inch square pans and line bottoms with waxed paper; grease paper.

Sift flour with baking powder and salt. Separate eggs. Beat yolks until light in color, then gradually beat in sugar and orange rind until thoroughly combined and thickened. Add enough water to the orange juice to make 1 cup. Add the flour mixture and liquid alternately to yolk mixture. beating after each addition. Wash beaters. Beat egg whites until they hold a peak. Add to batter and fold in gently at low speed until all patches of egg white disappear. Pour into prepared pans and bake 25 minutes or until cake tests done. Cool. Put cooled layers together with Orange Filling, then cover top with orange frosting.

ORANGE FILLING

1 egg
2 tablespoons cornstarch
¾ cup water
¾ cup granulated sugar

Juice and grated rind of 1 large orange
   (½ cup orange juice)
2 tablespoons lemon juice

Beat egg slightly. Mix cornstarch smooth with ¼ cup of the water. Stir cornstarch, remaining water, sugar, orange juice and rind, and lemon juice into egg and cook over a low heat, stirring constantly, until filling is smooth and thick. Do not boil.

ORANGE BUTTER FROSTING

¼ cup butter or margarine
2 cups confectioners' sugar

1-2 tablespoons orange juice
Grated rind of orange

Melt butter or margarine and mix with confectioners' sugar, orange juice and grated orange rind. Beat until smooth. Makes enough to cover top of cake.

FROSTINGS/GLAZES/TOPPINGS

AMARETTO GLAZE   Yield: 2½ cups

1 jar (12 ounces) orange marmalade
½ jar (5 ounces) apricot preserves
¼ cup Amaretto di Saronno liqueur

1 cup chopped, toasted almonds,
   divided

Combine orange marmalade, apricot preserves and liqueur in a small saucepan
and heat until melted. Drizzle 1 cup of glaze over cooled cake. Garnish top of cake
with ½ cup almonds. Allow cake to cool. Use remaining 1½ cups glaze and ½ cup
of almonds to garnish individual cake slices.

CHOCOLATE FUDGE FROSTING   Yield: fills and frosts 2 cake
                                      layers

1 tablespoon butter or margarine
3 (1 ounce) squares unsweetened
   chocolate
¼ cup milk

1 (3 ounce) package cream cheese
3 cups confectioners' sugar
½ teaspoon salt
1 teaspoon vanilla extract

Combine butter, chocolate and milk in a double boiler and heat until chocolate is
melted. Cool. In a large mixing bowl, combine cream cheese and cooled chocolate
mixture. Cream on medium speed for 1 minute. Turn to low speed, add confectioners' sugar, salt and vanilla extract. When ingredients are moistened, turn to
high speed and beat until mixture is light and fluffy, about 1-2 minutes. Scrape
sides of bowl as necessary. Spread onto cookies or cakes.

FLUFFY BUTTER FROSTING   Yield: Fills and frosts 2 cake layers

⅓ cup butter, softened
4 cups sifted confectioners' sugar
⅛ teaspoon salt

¼ cup milk
1½ teaspoons vanilla extract
1 tablespoon corn syrup

In large mixing bowl, cream butter on medium speed for 1 minute. Turn to low
speed and add confectioners' sugar, salt, milk and vanilla extract. When ingredients are moistened, add corn syrup and whip on high speed for 2 minutes.
Scrape sides of bowl as necessary. Spread on cookies or cake.

MOCHA FROSTING
Yield: Fills and frosts 2 cake layers

2 (1 ounce) squares unsweetened
   chocolate
1 teaspoon instant coffee
2 tablespoons hot water (160-180° F.)

6 tablespoons butter or margarine
2 cups confectioners' sugar
½ teaspoon vanilla extract

Melt chocolate in a double boiler. Set aside to cool. Dissolve coffee in hot water. Set aside to cool. In a large mixing bowl, cream butter on medium speed for 1 minute. Turn to low speed, add confectioners' sugar, chocolate, coffee and vanila extract. After ingredients are moistened, turn to high speed and continue beating for 1-2 minutes. Scrape sides of bowl as necessary. Mixture should be very creamy. Spread onto cookies or cake.

FLUFFY MERINGUE TOPPING
Yield: Tops 1 pie

3 egg whites
½ teaspoon vanilla extract

dash salt
½ cup granulated sugar

Allow egg whites to reach room temperature before mixing. Preheat oven to 400° F. In small mixing bowl, combine egg whites, vanilla extract and salt. Beat on high speed. Gradually add sugar and continue to beat until stiff peaks form. DO NOT OVERBEAT. Spread over pie filling, carefully sealing meringue over edge of pie crust (to prevent shrinking or weeping). Swirl with spatula or back of spoon. Bake for 5-10 minutes or until lightly browned.

WHIPPED CREAM TOPPING
Yield: Fills and frosts 2 cake layers

½ pint whipping cream
1 tablespoon confectioners' sugar
1 teaspoon vanilla extract

Chill whipping cream, beaters and small mixing bowl. Pour cream into chilled bowl. Beat on medium speed. Gradually add sugar and vanilla extract. Continue beating until soft, glossy peaks form. DO NOT OVERBEAT! Scrape sides of bowl as necessary. Spread onto cake. Cover and chill before serving.

CREME D'ORANGE
Yield: 2 cups

½ pint whipping cream
2 tablespoons frozen orange juice
   concentrate

2 tablespoons Cointreau liqueur

Place cream into small mixer bowl and beat on high speed until thick but not fully whipped. Add orange juice and Cointreau and continue beating until whipped. Serve as a dressing for a variety of fruit salads or as a topping for ginger cake or fruit compotes.

QUICK EGG WHITE FROSTING

Yield: Generously fills and frosts 2 cake layers

¾ cup light corn syrup
2 egg whites
Dash of salt

¼ cup granulated sugar
1½ teaspoons vanilla extract

Heat corn syrup in small saucepan to boil. In small mixing bowl, beat egg whites and salt on high speed for 30 seconds — until foamy. Gradually add sugar, continuing to beat until stiff peaks form — about 1 minute. Slowly add boiling corn syrup to egg white mixture. Add vanilla extract. Scrape sides of bowl as necessary. Continue beating until frosting becomes thick enough to spread — about 3 minutes. Spread onto cake in swirled pattern. Serve immediately.

CREAM CHEESE FROSTING

Yield: About 1 cup

3 tablespoons butter or margarine,
   softened
1 (3 ounce) package cream cheese,
   softened

1 cup confectioners' sugar
1 teaspoon vanilla extract

Combine all ingredients in small mixing bowl and beat on medium speed for 1 minute or until smooth.

VANILLA GLAZE

Yield: ½ cup glaze

1 cup confectioners' sugar
2 tablespoons milk

½ teaspoon vanilla extract
Food coloring, if desired

Mix all ingredients together in small mixing bowl on low speed for a few seconds until well blended.

VARIATION:

Melt one square unsweetened chocolate and add to above recipe.

VIENNA CHOCOLATE ICING   Yield: 1½ cups

4 squares unsweetened chocolate
1 cup confectioners' sugar
2 tablespoons hot water

2 eggs
6 tablespoons butter

In top of a double boiler, over boiling water, melt the chocolate. Remove pan from water. Beat into chocolate, at high speed, sugar and water. Continue beating, adding eggs, one at a time, then butter, 2 tablespoons at a time. Use to frost top and sides of Sacher Torte.

BUTTER CREAM FROSTING   Yield: about 3 cups

½ cup butter
⅛ teaspoon salt
3½ cups *sifted* confectioners' sugar

2 egg yolks, unbeaten
1 teaspoon vanilla extract
2 tablespoons rich milk or cream

Cream butter; add salt and part of sugar gradually, blending after each addition. Then add egg yolks and vanilla, blending well. Add remaining sugar alternately with milk, until of right consistency to spread, beating after each addition until smooth.

RUM BUTTER CREAM FROSTING: Use recipe for Butter Cream Frosting, eliminate vanilla and add 1 to 2 tablespoons of rum. You will not need to add as much milk.

Chapter Three
COOKIES AND SNACKS

CHOCOLATE FUDGE BROWNIES   Yield: 2 dozen

½ cup butter or margarine
4 ounces unsweetened chocolate
4 eggs
¼ teaspoon salt

2 cups granulated sugar
1 teaspoon vanilla extract
1 cup sifted all-purpose flour
1 cup chopped nuts

Preheat oven to 350° F. Thoroughly grease a 13 x 9 x 2-inch pan. Preheat oven to 350° F. Melt butter and chocolate in top of double boiler. Cool thoroughly. Beat eggs and salt until light in color and very foamy in texture. Gradually add the sugar and vanilla, beating at high speed. Remove beaters, and by hand stir in the chocolate mixture very quickly. Before it is completely combined, fold in the flour. While folding in the flour, add the nuts and gently fold in. Bake about 25 minutes. Do not cut until cool.

RAISIN CHOCOLATE CHIP COOKIES   Yield: 7-8 dozen

2 cups all-purpose flour
1 teaspoon baking soda
1 teaspoon cinnamon
¼ teaspoon salt
1 cup butter or margarine
1 cup granulated sugar
1 cup light brown sugar, packed

2 large eggs
1 teaspoon vanilla extract
2 cups quick cooking oatmeal
   (not instant)
1 (6 ounce) package (1 cup) semisweet
   chocolate pieces
1 cup dark seedless raisins

Stir together flour, baking soda, cinnamon and salt; set aside. Preheat oven to 375° F. In a large bowl beat together butter or margarine and sugars until very creamy; beat in eggs and vanilla. At low speed, stir in flour mixture gradually. By hand, stir in remaining ingredients. Use about 1 tablespoon for each cookie, and drop onto baking sheets, about 2 inches apart. Bake 9-12 minutes, or until crisp and golden brown. Cool on wire racks.

RAISIN WHOLE WHEAT COOKIES   Yield: 2-5 dozen

One cookie and a glass of milk make a very nourishing snack.

1 cup seedless raisins
1 cup shredded coconut
1 cup whole wheat flakes (cereal)
1 cup quick cooking oats (not instant)
2 cups whole wheat flour
½ teaspoon baking powder
½ teaspoon baking soda

½ teaspoon salt
¾ cup vegetable shortening
¾ cup brown sugar (packed)
¾ cup granulated sugar
2 eggs
1 teaspoon vanilla extract

Preheat oven to 375° F. Stir together raisins, coconut, cereal flakes, oats, whole wheat flour, baking powder, baking soda and salt. Set aside. In large mixing bowl beat together shortening and sugars. Beat in eggs and vanilla. At low speed, add about half the dry ingredients. Add the remainder by hand. It will form a very firm dough. Shape into balls and place on lightly greased baking sheets. Flatten each ball with the palm of your hand. These can be made in a conventional size, or make giant size balls to make only 2 dozen cookies. Bake 10-12 minutes.

OATMEAL RAISIN COOKIES   Yield: 4 dozen

1 cup granulated sugar
1 cup shortening
3 eggs
2 cups rolled oats (quick cooking)
2 cups all-purpose flour
½ teaspoon salt

½ teaspoon cinnamon
1 teaspoon baking powder
1 teaspoon baking soda
¼ cup molasses
1 cup raisins
½ cup chopped nuts

Preheat oven to 375° F. Grease cookie sheet. Place all ingredients in large mixing bowl. Blend on low speed for ½ minute then on medium speed until all ingredients are thoroughly combined. Drop by rounded tablespoonfuls onto prepared cookie sheets. Bake for 10-12 minutes or until bottom of cookie is lightly browned. Remove from cookie sheet and cool on wire racks.

SOFT MOLASSES COOKIES   Yield: 8½ dozen

2⅓ cups sifted all-purpose flour
1⅓ teaspoons baking soda
1 teaspoon cinnamon
1 teaspoon ginger
½ teaspoon salt
⅔ cup soft shortening

½ cup granulated sugar
1 egg
½ cup molasses
½ cup buttermilk
1 cup raisins

Set oven at 375° F. to preheat. Grease cookie sheets. Sift together flour, baking soda, cinnamon, ginger and salt. In large mixing bowl, combine shortening, sugar, egg and molasses. Cream on high speed for 1 minute. Turn to low speed. Add buttermilk and raisins. Gradually add flour mixture. Mix until thoroughly combined on medium speed. Drop by rounded teaspoonfuls onto prepared cookie sheets. Bake at 375° F. about 10-12 minutes. Remove from cookie sheets and cool on brown paper or paper toweling.

FUDGE DROPS   Yield: 3 dozen cookies

2 (1 ounce) squares unsweetened
   chocolate
1¾ cups sifted all-purpose flour
½ teaspoon baking soda
½ teaspoon salt
⅔ cup shortening

1 cup brown sugar, packed
1 egg
½ cup milk
1 teaspoon vanilla extract
1 cup chopped nuts

Preheat oven to 350° F. Grease cookie sheet. Melt chocolate in double boiler. Set aside to cool. Sift flour, baking soda and salt onto a sheet of waxed paper. In a large mixing bowl, add shortening and brown sugar. Cream on medium speed until well blended, about 1 minute. Add egg and chocolate and continue beating for 1 minute. Scrape sides of bowl as necessary. Turn to low speed and add flour mixture, milk and vanilla extract. After ingredients are moistened, turn to medium speed and beat for 1 minute. Scrape sides of bowl as necessary. Turn mixer OFF. Stir in nuts. Drop by rounded teaspoonfuls onto prepared cookie sheet. Bake for 8-10 minutes. Remove from cookie sheet and cool on wire racks.

Suggested frostings: Chocolate Fudge Frosting, Mocha Frosting

BANANA OATMEAL COOKIES

Yield: 3-4 dozen

Luscious big soft cookies — great with a glass of cold milk.

1½ cups all-purpose flour
1 teaspoon salt
½ teaspoon baking soda
½ teaspoon nutmeg
¾ teaspoon cinnamon
¾ cup margarine
1 cup granulated sugar

1 egg
1 cup mashed banana (2-3 bananas)
1 teaspoon vanilla or almond extract
1½ cups uncooked quick-cooking
  oatmeal (not instant)
½ cup chopped nuts
½ cup raisins

Preheat oven to 400° F. Grease cookie sheets. Sift flour, salt, baking soda, nutmeg and cinnamon. Beat together margarine, sugar and egg until very light. Beat in vanilla and mashed banana until smooth. At low speed, stir in flour mixture and oatmeal, then nuts and raisins.

Drop by teaspoonfuls onto greased cookie sheet. Bake 12-15 minutes.

SOUR CREAM COOKIES

Yield: 4 dozen

2 cups all-purpose flour
2½ teaspoons baking powder
¼ teaspoon baking soda
½ cup butter

1 cup granulated sugar
1 egg
½ cup sour cream
1 teaspoon lemon or vanilla extract

Grease cookie sheets. Preheat oven to 350° F. Sift together flour, baking powder and baking soda. Cream butter and sugar. Beat in egg; stir in sour cream and vanilla, then add dry ingredients. Drop from a teaspoon. Bake 8-10 minutes.

WALNUT CRESCENTS

Yield: 4 dozen

1 cup sifted all-purpose flour
⅛ teaspoon salt
½ cup butter, softened
½ cup granulated sugar

1 teaspoon vanilla extract
½ cup finely ground walnuts
1-2 teaspoons milk, if necessary
1 cup confectioners' sugar

Preheat oven to 300° F. Sift flour and salt onto a sheet of waxed paper. Combine butter, sugar and vanilla extract in a large mixing bowl. Cream on medium speed for 1 minute. Add flour and salt. Add walnuts and mix until well blended. Add milk, if necessary. Using level teaspoons of dough, roll into crescent shapes and place on ungreased cookie sheet. Bake for 20-25 minutes. Remove from cookie sheet and roll in confectioners' sugar. Cool on wire racks.

DATE DROPS   Yield: 5-6 dozen

2 cups all-purpose flour
1 cup butter, softened
½ cup granulated sugar
2 teaspoons vanilla extract

2 cups walnuts, finely chopped
1 cup dates, diced
2 cups confectioners' sugar

Preheat oven to 350° F. Grease a large cookie sheet. On a piece of waxed paper, sift flour. In a large mixing bowl, combine butter, sugar and vanilla extract. Cream on medium speed for 1 minute. Gradually add flour and continue beating until thoroughly combined, about 2 more minutes. Turn mixer to OFF. Stir in walnuts and dates. Roll teaspoonfuls of dough into balls and place approximately 1-inch apart on prepared cookie sheet. Bake for 15 minutes. Immediately remove cookies from cookie sheet and roll in confectioners' sugar. Let cool on wire racks.

RAINBOW BONBON TEA COOKIES   Yield: 20-25 cookies

½ cup soft butter
¾ cup sifted confectioners' sugar
2 teaspoons vanilla extract
½ teaspoon almond extract

1-2 tablespoons milk
1½ cups all-purpose flour
⅛ teaspoon salt
Food coloring, if desired

Possible fillings: candied cherries, chocolate chips, nut meats, dates.

Preheat oven to 350° F. In large mixing bowl, mix butter, sugar, flavorings and food coloring on high speed for ½ minute. Gradually add flour and salt to mix. Dough will be crumbly, if it appears too dry to mold, add milk. Wrap a level teaspoon of dough around desired filling. Place on ungreased cookie sheet 1-inch apart. Bake at 350° F. for 12-15 minutes. Cool on brown paper or paper toweling. Dip tops of cookie into tinted Vanilla glaze or Chocolate glaze. Top with nut meat or candies.

BUTTERSCOTCH REFRIGERATOR COOKIES   Yield: 3 dozen
cookies

2 cups sifted all-purpose flour
1 teaspoon baking powder
⅛ teaspoon baking soda
¼ teaspoon salt
½ cup butter, softened

1 cup brown sugar, firmly packed
1 egg
1 teaspoon vanilla extract
3 tablespoons milk
½ cup pecans, chopped

Sift onto a sheet of waxed paper, flour, baking powder, baking soda and salt. In a large mixing bowl, combine butter, brown sugar, egg and vanilla. Cream on medium speed for ½ minute. Turn to low speed, add flour mixture alternating with milk. Beat until well blended, scraping sides of bowl as necessary. Add pecans and continue beating until thoroughly combined. Form dough into two rolls 2 inches in diameter. Wrap in waxed paper. Refrigerate 1 hour. Preheat oven to 375° F. Slice cookie dough into slices ¼-inch thick. Place on ungreased cookie sheet and bake 10-12 minutes or until lightly browned. Cool on wire racks.

PEANUT BUTTER COOKIES   Yield: 4-5 dozen

2¼ cups all-purpose flour
2 teaspoons baking soda
¼ teaspoon salt
1 cup shortening
1 cup creamy-style peanut butter

1 cup brown sugar, firmly packed
½ cup granulated sugar
2 eggs
1 teaspoon vanilla extract
1 cup chopped peanuts

Preheat oven to 350° F. Sift onto a piece of waxed paper, flour, baking soda and salt. In a large mixing bowl, combine shortening, peanut butter, brown sugar and granulated sugar. Cream on medium speed for ½ minute. Add eggs and vanilla and continue beating until well blended. Scrape sides of bowl as necessary. Turn to low speed. Gradually add flour mixture. Beat until flour mixture is well blended; add peanuts and continue mixing until thoroughly combined. Roll into 1-inch balls. Place on ungreased cookie sheet; flatten with fork to form crisscross pattern. Bake for 10-12 minutes or until edges are golden brown. Cool on wire racks.

COCONUT MACAROONS   Yield: 3 dozen

2 egg whites
Dash of salt
¼ teaspoon vanilla extract

½ teaspoon almond extract
⅔ cup granulated sugar
1⅓ cups flaked coconut

Preheat oven to 325° F. Beat egg whites with salt, vanilla and almond extract on high speed adding sugar gradually until stiff peaks are formed, about 3 minutes. Fold in flaked coconut on low speed. Drop batter by rounded teaspoonfuls onto greased cookie sheet. Bake in a slow oven (325° F.) for 20 minutes.

SPRITZ COOKIES   Yield: 5 dozen

1 cup butter
¾ cup firmly packed brown sugar
1 egg yolk

½ teaspoon vanilla extract
¼ teaspoon salt
2 cups unsifted all-purpose flour

Set oven at 350° F. to preheat. In large mixing bowl cream butter and brown sugar together on high speed until light and fluffy — about ½ minute; combine with egg yolk, vanilla and salt. Blend in flour gradually on low speed. Remove beaters. Insert dough hooks. Knead dough until soft and pliable — about ½ minute. Press dough through cookiepress onto ungreased cookie sheets. May decorate, if desired, with decorator candies or colored sugar. Bake in 350° F. oven for 8 minutes or until lightly browned. Remove from cookie sheet and cool on brown paper or paper toweling.

SUGAR COOKIES   Yield: 5 dozen

2 cups sifted all-purpose flour
1 teaspoon baking powder
¼ teaspoon salt
⅛ teaspoon baking soda
⅛ teaspoon nutmeg
½ cup butter or margarine, softened

1½ cups granulated sugar, divided
1 egg
½ cup milk, divided
½ teaspoon vanilla extract
¼ teaspoon lemon extract

Sift flour, baking powder, salt, baking soda, and nutmeg onto a sheet of waxed paper. In a large mixing bowl, cream butter and 1 cup sugar on medium speed until light in color. Add egg and continue beating for 1 minute. Scrape sides of bowl as necessary. Turn to low speed, add flour mixture, 2 tablespoons milk, vanilla extract and lemon extract. When ingredients are moistened, turn to medium speed and beat until well blended, 1-2 minutes. Scrape sides of bowl as necessary. Cover bowl and refrigerate dough until easy to handle.

Preheat oven to 375° F. Grease cookie sheet. Remove dough from refrigerator. Roll out dough on a lightly floured board. For crisp cookies, roll to ⅛-inch thickness. For chewy cookies, roll dough to ¼-inch thickness. Cut with floured cookie cutter. Place on prepared cookie sheet. Brush with milk and sprinkle lightly with sugar. Bake for 10-12 minutes or until edges are light brown. Remove from cookie sheet and cool on wire racks.

SHORTBREAD   Yield: 2 dozen squares

2 cups sifted all-purpose flour
1 cup butter, softened

½ cup brown sugar, packed
½ cup chopped pecans

Preheat oven to 300° F. Sift flour onto a sheet of waxed paper. In large mixing bowl, cream butter and brown sugar on medium speed for 1 minute. Turn to low speed, add flour and beat until ingredients are moistened. Then turn to medium speed and beat until well blended, about 1-2 minutes. Scrape sides of bowl as necessary. Turn mixer to OFF. Stir in pecans. Pat dough into the bottom of a 13 x 9 x 2-inch pan. Prick shortbread with fork about every 2 inches. Bake for 20-25 minutes. Cut into 2-inch squares immediately after removing from oven. Allow to cool for 10 minutes before removing from pan. Finish cooling on wire racks.

DELIGHT SNACK BARS
butterscotch squares

Yield: 16 2-inch chocolate squares; 16 2-inch

½ cup margarine, softened
1 egg yolk
2 tablespoons water
1¼ cups sifted all-purpose flour

1 teaspoon granulated sugar
1 teaspoon baking powder
6 ounces chocolate chips
6 ounces butterscotch chips

TOPPING

2 eggs
¾ cup granulated sugar

6 tablespoons melted margarine
2 cups chopped pecans

Generously grease two 8 x 8 x 2-inch pans. Preheat oven to 350° F. Beat margarine, egg yolk and water on low speed until smooth, about 2 minutes. Sift together dry ingredients and mix with margarine mixture on low speed until thoroughly blended. Divide dough mixture in half. Place half of dough mixture in pan and press with fingers into a thin layer. Repeat with second pan. Bake at 350° F. for 10 minutes. **Prepare Topping:** Beat eggs until thick on medium speed. Beat in sugar. Add margarine, vanilla and nuts. Remove pans from oven. Sprinkle 6 ounces chocolate chips on top of one pan of dough. Sprinkle 6 ounces of butterscotch chips on top of second pan of dough. Return to oven for 2 minutes. Remove and spread chocolate chips and butterscotch chips over top. Pour half of topping mixture in each pan and spread mixture over top. Repeat for second pan. Bake at 350° F. for 30-35 minutes. Cut into squares.

DATE NUT SQUARES

Yield: 16 2-inch squares

2 eggs
½ cup brown sugar
½ teaspoon vanilla extract
½ cup all-purpose flour

½ teaspoon baking powder
½ teaspoon salt
1 cup nuts
2 cups chopped dates

Generously grease 8 x 8 x 2-inch square pan. Preheat oven to 325° F. In large bowl, beat eggs until foamy on medium speed for about ½ minute. Beat in sugar and vanilla on medium speed for ½ minute. Blend in flour, baking powder and salt on low speed for ½ minute. Mix in nuts and dates on low speed. Spread in greased pan. Bake at 325° F. for 40-45 minutes or until pulled from sides of pan. Cut into squares. May be sprinkled with powdered sugar. Cool. Remove from pan.

TRIPLE TREAT SNACK BARS

Yield: 32 squares

Crust

1 cup all-purpose flour
½ cup butter or margarine
¼ cup confectioners' sugar

Meringue Topping

2 egg whites
⅔ cup brown sugar, firmly packed
1 (6 ounce) package semi-sweet
   chocolate chips

Preheat oven to 350° F. In a small mixing bowl, combine flour, butter and confectioners' sugar. Mix on low speed until well blended. Pat dough into an even layer in an ungreased 8 x 8 x 2-inch square baking pan. Bake crust for 15-20 minutes until lightly browned.

While crust is baking, prepare Meringue Topping. In small mixing bowl, beat egg whites until foamy on high speed. Gradually add brown sugar and continue beating until stiff peaks form. DO NOT OVERBEAT.

Remove baked crusts from oven. Sprinkle chocolate chips over crust. Return to oven for 2 minutes. Remove from oven and spread chocolate over crust with a spatula. Spread Meringue Topping over chocolate, sealing it to edges of pan. Bake until meringue is light brown, approximately 20-25 minutes. Cool and cut into 1-inch squares.

LEMON BARS   Yield: 16

Crust

½ cup butter or margarine, softened
1¼ cups sifted all-purpose flour
¼ cup confectioners' sugar

Lemon Filling

¾ cup granulated sugar
2 eggs
1 tablespoon sifted all-purpose flour
¼ teaspoon baking powder

3 tablespoons freshly squeezed lemon
    juice
2 teaspoons grated lemon rind

Preheat oven to 350° F. In a small mixing bowl, combine butter, flour and confectioners' sugar. Mix on low speed until ingredients are moistened. Turn to medium speed and mix for 2 minutes, until mixture has a crumbly texture. Press mixture into an ungreased 8 x 8 x 2-inch square baking pan. Bake crust for 15-20 minutes until lightly browned.

While crust is baking, prepare Lemon Filling. In a large mixing bowl, combine sugar, eggs, flour, baking powder, lemon juice and lemon rind. Blend on low speed for 1-2 minutes. Scrape sides of bowl as necessary. Pour over partially baked crust and bake for an additional 15-20 minutes. Cool in pan on wire rack.

SNICKERDOODLES   Yield: 6 dozen

Kids love to make — and eat — these.

½ cup butter or margarine
½ cup vegetable shortening
1½ cups granulated sugar
2 eggs
2¼ cups all-purpose flour

2 teaspoons cream of tartar
1 teaspoon baking soda
¼ teaspoon salt
2 tablespoons granulated sugar
1 tablespoon cinnamon

Preheat oven to 400° F. In large mixer bowl, cream together thoroughly the butter, shortening, 1½ cups sugar and eggs. At low speed, blend in flour, cream of tartar, baking soda and salt, about 1 minute. Shape dough by rounded teaspoonfuls into 1-inch balls. Roll balls in mixture of sugar and cinnamon in a small bowl. Place 2-inches apart on ungreased baking sheets. Bake 8-10 minutes or until set. Remove from baking sheets immediately.

ALMOND COOKIES   Yield: 3½ dozen

1 cup vegetable shortening
1 cup granulated sugar
1 egg

2 teaspoons almond extract
3 cups sifted all-purpose flour
3½ dozen blanched whole almonds

Preheat oven to 350° F. Grease baking sheets. Cream together shortening, sugar, egg and almond extract until light and fluffy. At low speed, beat in 1 cup of flour. Work in the other 2 cups, one at a time, with a wooden mixing spoon. The dough will be very stiff. Form balls the size of small walnuts. Place on cookie sheets and press down to form thick rounds. Press an almond into the center of each cookie. Bake 8-10 minutes. Remove and cool on rack.

WHOOPIE PIES   Yield: 2 dozen

1¼ cups granulated sugar
½ cup unsweetened cocoa
2¼ cups all-purpose flour
1½ teaspoons baking soda
¼ teaspoon cream of tartar

¼ teaspoon salt
⅔ cup vegetable shortening
1 cup milk
2 eggs
2 teaspoons vanilla extract

Preheat oven to 350° F. Grease cookie sheets. Combine all dry ingredients in large bowl. Add shortening, milk, eggs and vanilla and beat thoroughly. Drop by level tablespoons onto cookie sheet, 2-inches apart. Bake 12-15 minutes. Fill when cooled.

FILLING

3 tablespoons all-purpose flour
½ cup milk
½ cup granulated sugar

4 teaspoons butter or margarine
½ cup vegetable shortening
½ teaspoon vanilla extract

Stir together in small saucepan the flour and milk. Cook until thick; cool. Add remaining ingredients. Beat at high speed 5-10 minutes, until very light and fluffy. Put two chocolate cookies together with a large spoonful of filling.

ITALIAN COOKIES

Yield: 5-6 dozen

4 cups all-purpose flour
1 cup granulated sugar
4 teaspoons baking powder
½ teaspoon salt

4 eggs, beaten
½ cup salad oil
2 teaspoons vanilla extract or
other flavoring*

Insert dough hooks. Put dry ingredients in large mixer bowl and stir together 30 seconds on low speed. Into the center of the dry ingredients pour eggs, oil and vanilla, and mix thoroughly on low speed. If dough is very soft, you may have to add flour. Preheat oven to 350° F. Form 1½-inch balls of dough and arrange on greased baking sheets. Bake 12-15 minutes or until lightly browned. Frost with vanilla glaze and decorate with multi-colored sprinkles.

* You may substitute anise or lemon flavoring and 2 teaspoons grated orange rind.

MOLASSES CRISPIES

Yield: 5 dozen

¾ cup shortening
2 cups sifted all-purpose flour
2 teaspoons baking soda
½ teaspoon cloves
½ teaspoon ginger
1 teaspoon cinnamon

½ teaspoon salt
1 cup granulated sugar
¼ cup molasses
1 egg
Granulated sugar

Melt shortening in pan; remove from heat and cool. Sift together flour, baking soda, cloves, ginger, cinnamon, salt. Set aside. When shortening is cool, pour into mixer bowl; add sugar, molasses and egg, and beat well. At low speed, stir in dry ingredients. Chill dough for 1 hour. Preheat oven to 375° F. Roll dough into 1-inch balls. Roll in granulated sugar. Put on lightly greased cookie sheet 2-inches apart — they will flatten out. Bake 10-12 minutes or until lightly browned. Remove to wire racks to cool.

COCOA BROWNIES   Yield: 2 dozen

1½ cups sifted all-purpose flour
½ cup cocoa
½ teaspoon baking powder
Pinch of salt
½ cup butter or margarine, softened

½ cup shortening
2 cups granulated sugar
4 eggs
1 teaspoon vanilla extract
1 cup chopped nuts

Preheat oven to 350° F. Grease and dust with flour a 13 x 9 x 2-inch pan. Sift flour, cocoa, baking powder and salt onto a sheet of waxed paper. In a large mixing bowl, cream butter, shortening and sugar on medium speed for 1 minute. Add eggs and continue mixing until well blended, about 2 minutes. Scrape sides of bowl as necessary. Turn to low speed and gradually add flour mixture. When ingredients are moistened, add vanilla extract. Turn to medium speed and continue mixing for 1 more minute. Scrape sides of bowl as necessary. Stir in nuts using a spoon. Pour into prepared pan and bake for 25-30 minutes. Cool in pan on a wire rack.

CHOCOLATE CHIP COOKIES   Yield: 6 dozen

2¼ cups sifted all-purpose flour
1 teaspoon salt
1 teaspoon baking soda
1 cup butter or margarine, softened
1 cup brown sugar, packed

⅔ cup granulated sugar
2 eggs
1 teaspoon vanilla extract
1 (12 ounce) package chocolate chips
1 cup chopped nuts

Preheat oven to 375° F. Grease cookie sheet. Sift flour, salt and baking soda onto a sheet of waxed paper. In a large mixing bowl, cream butter, brown sugar, and granulated sugar on medium speed for 1 minute. Add eggs and vanilla extract and continue beating for 2 minutes. Scrape sides of bowl as necessary. Turn to low speed and add flour mixture. When ingredients are moistened, turn to medium speed and continue beating for 1 minute, until ingredients are well blended. Scrape sides of bowl as necessary. Turn mixer OFF. Stir in chocolate chips and nuts. Drop by rounded teaspoonfuls onto prepared cookie sheet. Bake for 8-10 minutes. Cool on wire racks.

SUGAR SNAPS   Yield: 12 dozen

4 cups unsifted all-purpose flour
1 teaspoon salt
1 teaspoon baking soda
1 teaspoon cream of tartar
1 cup butter or margarine
1 cup salad oil

1 cup confectioners' sugar
1 cup granulated sugar
2 eggs
1 teaspoon vanilla extract
Extra granulated sugar

In medium bowl combine first four ingredients; set aside. In large mixer bowl with mixer at medium speed, cream butter or margarine, salad oil and confectioners' sugar and granulated sugar until very light and fluffy. Add eggs one at a time and vanilla and continue mixing until just combined. Wrap and refrigerate dough at least 2 hours.

Preheat oven to 350° F. Grease cookie sheets. Shape dough into 1-inch balls. Roll in additional granulated sugar. Place on cookie sheets. Press each ball down with a fork. Bake 10-12 minutes or until lightly browned. Remove immediately to wire racks to cool.

Note: This recipe can be cut in half. Baked cookies can be frozen in airtight bags and will keep well.

PINEAPPLE FILLED COOKIES   Yield: 3-4 dozen

FILLING

1 pound (14 ounce) can crushed
    pineapple
½ cup water

¼ cup granulated sugar
1 tablespoon cornstarch
2 egg yolks

Blend filling ingredients together in medium saucepan and cook until very thick. Cool.

1 cup shortening
1½ cups granulated sugar
2 eggs
½ cup milk

1½ teaspoons vanilla extract
5 cups all-purpose flour
¼ teaspoon salt
1 teaspoon baking soda

Preheat oven to 350° F. Grease cookie sheets. Cream together shortening and sugar; beat in eggs. At low speed, beat in milk and vanilla. Stir together flour, salt and baking soda, and gradually stir in. The last additions of flour should be made by hand. Chill 1 hour. Roll out thin and cut into 3½-inch circles. Put a spoonful of pineapple filling on center of a round, cover with another and crimp edges with a fork. Make a slit on top of each cookie. Bake 10-12 minutes or until lightly browned.

LITHUANIAN NECKTIES   Yield: 8-10 dozen

A prize winning recipe.

3 cups all-purpose flour
½ teaspoon salt
6 eggs, separated
Shortening for frying

½ teaspoon almond extract
1 teaspoon vanilla extract
½ cup confectioners' sugar

Sift together flour and salt and set aside. Put shortening in pan ready to melt, but do not begin to heat until ready to roll out the dough. An electric frypan is perfect for frying these cookies — with shortening enough for a depth of 1½-2-inches.

Beat egg whites until stiff, beating in confectioners' sugar. Beat egg yolks until very thick and lemon colored. Fold the whites gently into the yolks; fold in extracts. Insert dough hooks and at low speed very gently fold in the flour. Knead the dough until it leaves sides of the bowl, adding more flour if necessary. Divide dough into three or four pieces; cover each piece, and keep covered till ready to use (overturn a bowl on it). Using one piece at a time, roll out dough as thin as possible, adout ⅛-inch thick. Cut into strips 3-inches long and 1-inch wide. In the center of each strip make a lengthwise slit about 1-inch long. Pull one end of the strip through the slit to form a "knot." Fry in deep fat until brown. Sprinkle with confectioners' sugar.

HERMITS   Yield: 3 dozen

3 cups all-purpose flour
1 teaspoon cinnamon
½ teaspoon salt
1 teaspoon baking soda
1 cup granulated sugar

½ cup salad oil
½ cup milk
½ cup molasses
¾ cup raisins
½ cup chopped nuts

Note: Yes — there are no eggs in these.

Preheat oven to 350° F. Grease a 10 x 15-inch jelly roll pan. Sift together the first four ingredients and set aside. At medium speed beat sugar and oil thoroughly. Add sifted dry ingredients alternately with milk and molasses, beating thoroughly on low speed. Stir in raisins and nuts. Drop by rounded teaspoonfuls onto prepared pan. Bake 20-25 minutes. Sprinkle with granulated sugar if desired.

VARIATION

You can vary amount and type of fruit: use dates, candied fruits, more or less depending on what you like.

Chapter Four
PASTRIES AND PUFFS

PASTRY TIPS

— Use your mixer to full advantage. Stir together flour and salt at low speed; add shortening and cut in at low speed. It will take only a minute or two. Add water, another 30 seconds, and your crust is ready to be rolled out.

— Remove ball of dough from bowl, flatten out and place on a floured pastry cloth, floured board or lightly floured piece of waxed paper. If using waxed paper, cover with another piece of waxed paper and roll.

— Always roll from the center of the pastry to the edges. Do not bear down hard on the dough — let the rolling pin do the job.

— Fold rolled dough into quarters and place in pie pan. Then, just unfold it very gently to fit pan.

— For a LATTICE TOP, roll dough into a rectangle as wide as the pie pan. Cut strips ½-inch wide and weave them on top of the filling. Trim even with the bottom crust and seal edges.

— Fit pie crust loosely in the pan; do not stretch at all.

— Reroll trimmings from crust, sprinkle with sugar and cinnamon and bake a few minutes for an extra little treat.

PASTRY FOR DOUBLE CRUST PIE

2 cups all-purpose flour
1 teaspoon salt

⅔ cup vegetable shortening
4 or 5 tablespoons very cold water

Combine flour and salt in mixing bowl. Insert dough hooks or use beaters and stir at low speed 30 seconds. Add shortening and cut in at low speed for about 2 minutes or until mixture is consistency of coarse meal. Add water and stir together with dough hooks or beaters just until all of the dough clumps together and forms a ball.

PASTRY FOR SINGLE CRUST PIE

1 cup all-purpose flour
½ teaspoon salt

⅓ cup vegetable shortening
2 to 2½ tablespoons very cold water

Proceed as for double crust pie.

PIE SHELLS

Unbaked: Roll out the recipe for 1-crust pie to ⅛-inch thickness. Ease into pie pan. Fold under the edges of the crust and press into an upright rim. Refrigerate until ready to fill.

Baked: Make pie shell as for Unbaked Pie shell, but prick the entire surface evenly and closely with a 4-tined fork. Be sure to do sides as well as bottom. Refrigerate. Preheat oven to 450° F. and bake crust 10-15 minutes or until lightly browned. Cool before filling.

CRUMB CRUSTS

Graham Cracker Crust

1⅓ cups graham cracker crumbs
    (16-18)
¼ cup granulated sugar
¼ cup soft butter or margarine
¼ teaspoon nutmeg or cinnamon
    (optional)

Combine crumbs, sugar, butter and nutmeg. Blend well. Press crumbs evenly on bottom and sides of 9-inch pie pan, making a small rim. Bake in preheated 375° F. oven 8-10 minutes or until lightly browned. Cool before filling.

Unbaked Graham Cracker Crust

Make recipe for Graham Cracker Crust. Refrigerate at least 1 hour.

Chocolate Wafer Crumb Crust

1⅓ cups fine chocolate wafer crumbs
    (about 18)
3 tablespoons soft butter or margarine

Vanilla Wafer Crumb Crust

1⅓ cups fine vanilla wafer crumbs
    (about 24)
¼ cup soft butter or margarine

Gingersnap Crumb Crust

1⅓ cups fine gingersnap crumbs
    (about 20)
6 tablespoons soft butter or margarine

Make all these crumb crusts the same as Graham Cracker Crust.

OATMEAL NUT CRUST   Yield: one 9-inch pie crust

1 cup uncooked rolled oats   ⅔ cup very finely chopped walnuts
3 tablespoons brown sugar   ⅓ cup butter or margarine

Preheat oven to 350° F. Spread oats in large, shallow pan; bake 10 minutes to toast. Toss with sugar, nuts and melted butter. Press evenly on bottom and side of 9-inch pie plate. Bake 8-10 minutes. Cool and fill.

MERINGUE CRUST   Yield: 1 (9-inch) meringue

4 egg whites   Pinch of salt
½ teaspoon cream of tartar   1 cup granulated sugar

Beat egg whites, cream of tartar and a pinch of salt in a large mixer bowl on high speed until stiff — about 1 minute. Slowly beat in granulated sugar, beating 1 minute longer. Spread over bottom and up sides to rim of well-greased 9-inch pie plate, making bottom ¼-inch thick, side 1-inch thick. Bake 40 minutes at 300° F. or until brown and crisp. Fill with ice cream, top with sweetened berries or fill with Parfait pie filling.

CREAM PIE   Yield: 6-8 servings

⅓ cup sifted all-purpose flour or ¼   2 tablespoons butter or margarine
   cup cornstarch   ½ teaspoon vanilla extract
⅔ cup granulated sugar   1 baked 9-inch pastry shell
¼ teaspoon salt   3 stiffly beaten egg whites
2 cups milk, scalded   6 tablespoons granulated sugar
3 slightly beaten egg yolks

Preheat oven to 350° F. Mix flour, ⅔ cup sugar and salt; gradually add milk. Cook over moderate heat, stirring constantly, until mixture thickens and boils. Cook 2 minutes; remove from heat.

Add small amount to egg yolks; stir into remaining hot mixture; cook 1 minute, stirring constantly. Add butter, vanilla; cool slightly. Pour into baked pastry shell. Cover with meringue made of egg whites beaten stiff with the 6 tablespoons granulated sugar. Bake 15-20 minutes or until meringue is golden brown. Instead of a meringue, you can top with one cup heavy cream, whipped until stiff and sweetened with 2 tablespoons sugar.

VARIATIONS

Banana Cream Pie: Cover pie shell with sliced bananas; add filling. Top with whipped cream, garnish with banana slices that have been dipped in orange juice or lemon juice.

Butterscotch Pie: Substitute 1 cup brown sugar for ⅔ cup granulated sugar; increase butter to 3 tablespoons.

Chocolate: Increase sugar to 1 cup; melt two 1-ounce squares unsweetened chocolate in scalded milk.

LEMON MERINGUE PIE   Yield: 6-8 servings

1½ cups granulated sugar
⅓ cup plus 1 tablespoon cornstarch
1½ cups water
3 egg yolks, slightly beaten

3 tablespoons butter or margarine
Grated peel of 1 lemon
⅔ cup freshly squeezed lemon juice
1 baked (9-inch) pastry shell

Preheat oven to 400° F. Mix sugar and cornstarch in small saucepan. Gradually add water. Cook over medium heat, stirring constantly. Allow mixture to boil for 1-1½ minutes. Gradually stir half of the hot mixture into the egg yolks. Pour egg yolk mixture back into the pan. Allow mixture to boil for 1-1½ minutes, while stirring constantly. Remove from heat, stir in butter, lemon peel and lemon juice. Pour into prepared pastry shell.

Suggested Topping: Fluffy meringue topping

MERINGUE TIPS

— Be certain to beat the egg whites long enough to dissolve the sugar completely.
— Pile meringue on hot filling, and spread so that the meringue touches the pie shell all around.

PUMPKIN PIE   Yield: 8-10 servings

3 eggs
1½ cups cooked or canned pumpkin
1 (13 ounce) can evaporated milk
½ cup brown sugar, firmly packed
½ cup granulated sugar
1½ teaspoons cinnamon

½ teaspoon ginger
½ teaspoon nutmeg
⅛ teaspoon salt
1 teaspoon vanilla extract
1 unbaked deep dish pastry shell,
    chilled

Preheat oven to 450° F. In a large mixing bowl, beat eggs on high speed about ½ minute. Stop mixer and add pumpkin, evaporated milk, brown sugar, granulated sugar, cinnamon, ginger, nutmeg, salt and vanilla extract. Beat on medium speed until blended, about 1½ minutes. Scrape sides of the bowl as necessary. Pour into prepared pastry shell. Bake for 10 minutes, then reduce heat to 350° F. and bake for 45 minutes, or until knife inserted into center of pie comes out clean. Serve slightly warmed.

Suggested Topping: Whipped cream topping

PECAN PIE   Yield: 6-8 servings

2 eggs
¾ cup granulated sugar
1 cup light corn syrup
2 tablespoons butter or margarine,
    melted

1 tablespoon all-purpose flour
1 teaspoon vanilla extract
⅛ teaspoon salt
1¼ cups pecan halves
1 unbaked (9-inch) pastry shell

Preheat oven to 400° F. Place eggs in small mixing bowl. Beat on medium speed until light, approximately 15 seconds. Turn to low. Add sugar, corn syrup, butter, flour, vanilla, salt, and continue beating until well blended about 1-2 minutes. Stir in pecan halves and pour into prepared pie shell. Bake for 15 minutes. Reduce oven temperature to 350° F. and bake for an additional 30-35 minutes, or until knife inserted into center of pie comes out clean. Cool before serving.

Suggested Topping: Whipped cream topping

GRASSHOPPER PIE   Yield: 6-8 servings

2 packages (3 ounces each) or 1 package (6 ounces) lime gelatin
3 tablespoons granulated sugar
Dash salt
2 cups boiling water
½ cup cold water
⅓ cup crème de cacao liqueur

⅓ cup crème de menthe liqueur
1½ teaspoons vanilla extract
2 egg whites
1 envelope whipped topping mix or 1 cup whipping cream
½ cup semi-sweet chocolate morsels
9 or 10-inch chocolate crumb crust

In large mixing bowl dissolve gelatin, 1 tablespoon sugar and salt in boiling water. Add cold water, liqueurs and vanilla. Chill until slightly thickened. In small mixer bowl, beat egg whites on high speed until foamy — about ½ minute. Gradually add remaining sugar, beating after each addition until well blended. Then beat until meringue will stand in shiny, soft peaks — about 2 minutes. Remove from bowl and set aside. Wash and dry small bowl and beaters and whip topping mix as directed on package, omitting vanilla, or whip cream in small bowl on high speed until thickened. Remove ½ cup gelatin mixture from larger mixing bowl and set aside. Fold meringue and prepared topping or whipped cream into remaining gelatin mixture on low speed. Mix just long enough to combine ingredients. Pour mixture into prepared crust. Drizzle the reserved clear gelatin over the top of pie; pull spoon through a zigzag course to marble. Sprinkle chocolate chips over top of pie. Chill for several hours until firm.

BLACK BOTTOM PIE   Yield: 6-8 servings

⅔ cup granulated sugar, divided
1 tablespoon cornstarch
4 egg yolks, well beaten
2 cups milk, scalded
¾ teaspoon vanilla extract
1 (6 ounce) package semi-sweet chocolate chips

1 (9-inch) prepared pastry shell
1 envelope (1 tablespoon) unflavored gelatin
¼ cup cold water
1 teaspoon rum extract or 4 tablespoons light rum
4 egg whites

Blend ⅓ cup sugar and cornstarch in a small bowl and set aside. Add egg yolks to a small saucepan. While stirring constantly, add scalded milk and sugar mixture to egg yolks. Cook over medium heat, stirring occasionally, until custard thickens. Remove from heat and add vanilla extract. Pour 1 cup of custard mixture into small bowl. Add chocolate chips and stir until melted. Pour into prepared pastry shell and chill. Meanwhile, soften gelatin in cold water. Add softened gelatin to remaining hot custard and stir until dissolved. Stir in rum extract. Chill until slightly thickened. In a large mixing bowl, beat egg whites on high speed. Gradually add remaining ⅓ cup sugar. Continue beating until soft peaks form. Turn to low speed and fold in rum/custard mixture. Chill, if necessary, until mixture mounds. Remove pie shell from refrigerator. Pile rum/custard layer over chocolate layer and chill until set. Garnish with chopped nuts, if desired.

Suggested Topping: Chopped nuts

KEY LIME PIE   Yield: 6-8 servings

1 package (3 ounces) lime gelatin
¾ cup boiling water
1 tablespoon grated lime rind
Juice of two limes or ½ cup lime juice
2 egg yolks

1⅓ cups (15 ounces) sweetened
  condensed milk
¼ teaspoon aromatic bitters
2 drops green food coloring
2 egg whites
1 baked 9-inch pastry shell, cooled

Dissolve gelatin in boiling water. Add lime rind and juice to the gelatin. In large mixing bowl, beat egg yolks for a few seconds on low speed. Slowly add gelatin, condensed milk, bitters and food coloring and continue mixing on low speed until thoroughly blended. Chill mixture until slightly thickened. In small bowl beat egg whites on high speed until stiff peaks form. Fold egg whites into gelatin mixture on low speed. Pour into pastry shell. Chill until firm. Garnish with prepared whipped cream topping and lime slices or shaved chocolate, if desired.

Suggested Topping: Whipped cream topping, shaved chocolate

CHOCOLATE BAVARIAN PIE   Yield: 6-8 servings

3 slightly beaten egg yolks
½ cup granulated sugar
¼ teaspoon salt
1 cup milk, scalded
1 tablespoon (1 envelope) unflavored
  gelatin

¼ cup cold water
1 teaspoon vanilla extract
3 stiffly beaten egg whites
1 cup heavy cream
1 9-inch chocolate wafer crumb crust

Combine egg yolks, sugar and salt; slowly add milk. Cook in double boiler until mixture coats spoon. Soften gelatin in cold water; stir into hot mixture. Chill until partially set. Add vanilla. Fold in egg whites and whipped cream. Pour into chocolate wafer crust. Sprinkle with ¼ cup wafer crumbs. Chill.

BRANDY ALEXANDER PIE

Yield: 6-8 servings

1 envelope unflavored gelatin
½ cup cold water
⅔ cup granulated sugar
⅛ teaspoon salt
3 eggs, separated
¼ cup brandy

¼ cup crème de cacao
2 cups heavy cream, whipped
1 9-inch graham cracker crust
Grated chocolate or chocolate curls
    for garnish

Sprinkle gelatin over the cold water in a saucepan. Add ⅓ cup of the sugar, the salt and egg yolks. Stir to blend. Heat over low heat while stirring until gelatin dissolves and mixture thickens. Do not boil. Remove from heat and stir in the brandy and crème de cacao. Chill until mixture starts to mound slightly.

Beat egg whites until stiff. Gradually beat in the remaining sugar and fold into the thickened mixture. Fold in 1 cup of the whipped cream. Turn into the crust. Chill for several hours or overnight. Garnish with remaining cream and chocolate.

CHOCOLATE CHIFFON PIE

Yield: 6-8 servings

1 tablespoon unflavored gelatin
½ cup cold water
2 (1 ounce) squares unsweetened
    chocolate, melted
4 eggs, separated
¾ cup granulated sugar

Dash of salt
1½ teaspoons vanilla extract
1 vanilla wafer pie shell
1 recipe whipped cream topping
    (page 68)
1 baked 9-inch pastry shell

In large mixing bowl soften gelatin in cold water for 5 minutes. Add melted chocolate, egg yolks, ½ cup sugar, salt and vanilla. Beat on medium speed until thoroughly combined. Cool until mixture begins to thicken. In small mixing bowl beat egg whites on high speed until foamy. Slowly add remaining ¼ cup sugar and continue beating until stiff peaks are formed. Fold egg whites into gelatin mixture on low speed just long enough to combine ingredients. Pour into pie shell and chill until firm. Spread with whipped cream topping before serving.

LEMON CHIFFON PIE   Yield: 6-8 servings

½ cup lemon juice
½ teaspoon salt
¼ cup granulated sugar
4 egg yolks, beaten
1 tablespoon gelatin
¼ cup cold water

1 teaspoon grated lemon rind
4 egg whites
½ cup granulated sugar
1 cup whipped cream, sweetened
1 baked 9-inch pie shell

Combine lemon juice, salt, sugar and egg yolks in saucepan and cook, stirring constantly, over low heat until of custard consistency. Add gelatin which has been softened in cold water. Stir until the gelatin is dissolved. Add lemon rind. Cool. Refrigerate until it begins to thicken and mounds when dropped from spoon. At high speed, beat egg whites until stiff; beat in the ½ cup sugar. Fold into lemon mixture; fill pie shell and refrigerate. Before serving, mound sweetened whipped cream on top.

PUMPKIN CHIFFON PIE   Yield: 6-8 servings

2 envelopes unflavored gelatin
⅓ cup light brown sugar, firmly
    packed
½ teaspoon salt
2 teaspoons pumpkin pie spice
1½ tablespoons dark molasses
3 egg yolks, slightly beaten
½ cup milk

1 can (1 pound) pumpkin
3 egg whites
½ cup granulated sugar
1 cup heavy cream, whipped
Whipped cream
Walnut halves
One Oatmeal Nut crust

In medium saucepan, combine gelatin, brown sugar, salt and spice; mix well. Add molasses, egg yolks, milk and pumpkin, stirring until well combined. Bring to boiling, stirring. Remove from heat; turn into large bowl. Refrigerate, covered, until firm — 1½-2 hours.

In large bowl of electric mixer, beat egg whites at high speed until foamy. Add sugar, 2 tablespoons at a time, beating well after each addition. Continue to beat until stiff peaks form when beater is slowly raised. Then, with same beaters, beat pumpkin mixture until smooth. With wire whisk or rubber scraper, gently fold egg white mixture and whipped cream into pumpkin mixture just until combined. Turn into pie shell, mounding high in center. (If filling seems too soft to mound in pie shell, refrigerate it for 10 minutes; then turn filling into pie shell.) Refrigerate until firm — at least 2 hours.

To serve: Garnish with whipped cream put through pastry bag with rosette tube. Then top with walnut halves.

PEANUT BUTTER CREAM CHEESE PIE

Yield: 5-7 servings

2 (3 ounce) packages softened
cream cheese
¾ cup sifted confectioners' sugar
½ cup peanut butter

2 tablespoons milk
1 envelope dessert topping mix
1 8-inch graham cracker pie shell
Coarsely chopped peanuts

In small mixing bowl beat together cream cheese and sugar until light and fluffy. Add the peanut butter and milk, beating until smooth and creamy. Prepare dessert topping mix according to package directions; fold into peanut butter mixture. Turn into prepared crust. Chill 5-6 hours or overnight. Garnish with coarsely chopped peanuts.

Note: This is also delicious if served frozen.

CHERRY 'N' ICE CREAM PIE

Yield: 6-8 servings

½ pint whipping cream
1 (1 pound 1 ounce) dark, pitted
cherries in heavy syrup, drained
⅔ cup granulated sugar
1 teaspoon vanilla extract

¼ teaspoon almond extract
1-2 drops red food coloring
1 quart vanilla ice cream, softened
1 baked 9-inch pastry shell, cooled

Chill cream, beaters, and small mixing bowl. Meanwhile, cut cherries in half and set aside. Pour cream into chilled bowl. Beat on high speed. Gradually add sugar. Continue beating until stiff peaks form, scraping sides of bowl as necessary. Add vanilla extract, almond extract and food coloring. DO NOT OVERBEAT. Stop mixer and fold in cherries. Spoon into prepared pastry shell, alternating with ice cream. Freeze for at least two hours before serving.

Suggested Topping: Chopped nuts.

FROZEN BERRY PIE

Yield: 6-8 servings

1 package (10 ounces) frozen
raspberries or strawberries
¾ cup granulated sugar
2 egg whites, at room temperature

1 tablespoon lemon juice
⅛ teaspoon salt
1 cup whipping cream, whipped
Baked 9-inch pie shell

Thaw berries. Combine berries, sugar, egg whites, lemon juice and salt. Beat for 12-15 minutes at high speed, or until very stiff. Fold in whipped cream. Mound in baked pie shell. Freeze until firm. Garnish with mint sprigs.

INDIVIDUAL CHEESECAKE TARTS   Yield: 24

4 tablespoons melted butter or
  margarine
¾ cup graham cracker crumbs
  (8-9 crackers)
¾ cup granulated sugar

2 eggs
1 teaspoon vanilla extract
1 tablespoon lemon juice
2 (8 ounce) packages cream cheese

Place foil liners in muffin tins. Combine melted butter or margarine with graham cracker crumbs; divide evenly among 24 muffin cups and press firmly to cover bottom of cup. Preheat oven to 350° F. Combine remaining ingredients in medium bowl and beat at medium speed until smooth. Spoon into muffin cups. Bake 10 minutes.

TOPPING

1 pint dairy sour cream
2 tablespoons granulated sugar
1 teaspoon vanilla extract

Increase oven temperature to 400° F. Combine sour cream, sugar and vanilla in small bowl. Beat well at medium speed. Spoon on tarts and bake for 3 minutes. If desired, spoon on blueberry, cherry or pineapple pie filling. One can is sufficient for all the tarts.

RICOTTA PIE   Yield: 6-8 servings

CRUST

2 cups all-purpose flour
2 tablespoons granulated sugar
½ teaspoon baking powder
⅛ teaspoon salt

1 egg
¼ cup vegetable oil
Water, if needed

FILLING

¾ cup granulated sugar
2 eggs
Grated peel of a medium-sized orange

1 pound ricotta cheese
½ cup semi-sweet chocolate chips

Preheat oven to 350° F.

For crust: Combine dry ingredients in a bowl. Beat together egg and oil; stir into dry ingredients with a fork. The dough should form a ball. If dry, add cold water as necessary. Divide in half. Roll out half to fit a 9-inch pie plate. Roll out other half and cut into strips to make a lattice top crust.

For filling: At medium speed of electric mixer beat together sugar, eggs, orange rind, and ricotta cheese. Stir in chocolate bits by hand. Pour into crust; top with a lattice crust. Bake 45 minutes.

INNKEEPER'S PIE   Yield: 10 servings

9-inch pie shell
2 squares unsweetened chocolate
1½ cups water
⅔ cup granulated sugar
¼ cup butter or margarine
2 teaspoons vanilla extract
1 cup sifted all-purpose flour

¾ cup granulated sugar
1 teaspoon baking powder
½ teaspoon salt
¼ cup soft shortening
½ cup milk
1 egg
½ cup chopped walnuts

Preheat oven to 350° F. Fit pie crust into deep 9-inch pan and refrigerate while making filling. Melt chocolate in water in saucepan; add ⅔ cup sugar. Bring to a boil, stirring constantly. Add butter and 1½ teaspoons vanilla. Remove from heat. Combine flour, ¾ cup sugar, baking powder and salt in bowl; add shortening, milk, remaining vanilla. Beat at medium speed for 2 minutes. Add egg; beat for 2 minutes longer. Pour into prepared pie shell. Stir chocolate mixture; pour over batter slowly. Sprinkle with walnuts. Bake 55-60 minutes or until tooth pick inserted into center comes out clean. Serve slightly warm with topping.

TOPPING

1 cup whipping cream
2 tablespoons granulated sugar
1 teaspoon vanilla extract

Whip cream, adding sugar, 1 tablespoon at a time. Add vanilla; beat until fluffy. Pile cream around edge of pie. Garnish with additional chopped walnuts. Serve immediately.

CRANBERRY CHIFFON PIE   Yield: 6-8 servings

1 baked 9-inch pastry shell
1 envelope (1 tablespoon) unflavored
  gelatin
½ cup cold water
2 cups (½ pound) fresh cranberries
2 egg whites

1 cup granulated sugar
1 tablespoon lemon juice
¼ teaspoon salt
1 cup heavy cream
1 tablespoon granulated sugar

Prepare and bake pastry shell; cool. Soften gelatin in water. In saucepan combine cranberries and gelatin. Bring to boil; simmer 5 minutes, stirring often. Cool.

In large mixer bowl, combine egg whites, sugar, lemon juice, salt and cranberry mixture. Beat until mixture holds firm peaks, about 6-8 minutes. Pile into pastry shell. Chill 4-5 hours. Whip cream and 1 tablespoon sugar; spoon on top of pie.

PUMPKIN ICE CREAM PIE

Yield: 6-8 servings

1 9-inch pie shell or Ginger Snap
   Crumb Crust
1 pint vanilla ice cream
2 tablespoons cut up crystallized
   ginger
1 cup canned or mashed cooked
   pumpkin
1 cup granulated sugar

1 teaspoon pumpkin pie spice
½ teaspoon ginger
¼ teaspoon salt
½ cup finely chopped walnuts
1 cup heavy cream

Stir ice cream to soften. Quickly fold in crystallized ginger and spread in pie shell.
Freeze until ice cream is solid. Stir together pumpkin, sugar, pumpkin pie spice,
ginger, salt and walnuts. Whip cream until stiff and fold into pumpkin mixture.
Pour over ice cream. Freeze at least several hours. About 20 minutes before serving, remove from freezer and place in refrigerator to soften.

Chapter Five
MIXER MAIN DISHES

HAM LOAF   Yield: 6 servings

2 pounds cooked ham	1 teaspoon prepared mustard
1 pound ground pork	1 tablespoon vinegar
¾ cup soft bread crumbs	8 slices canned pineapple
1 egg	Maraschino Cherries
⅛ teaspoon pepper	¼ cup brown sugar
¾ cup milk	2 tablespoons butter

Attach grinder to mixer, insert meat cutter plate. Cut up the ham into cubes and put through the grinder. Combine with pork, bread crumbs, egg, pepper, milk, mustard and vinegar. Divide mixture in half. Grease two small 5-inch loaf pans and line with waxed paper. Place pineapple rings on bottom and sides of pan; put cherry in center of each ring. Pack the ham mixture into pans. Chill 1 hour. Unmold into shallow roasting pan. Remove waxed paper; cover with mixture of brown sugar and butter. Bake in 350° F. 1 hour.

POPOVERED CHICKEN   Yield: 4 servings

1 (3 pound) broiler-fryer	5 large eggs
½ cup all-purpose flour	2 cups all-purpose flour
½ teaspoon salt	2 cups milk
¼ teaspoon pepper	¾ teaspoon salt
2 tablespoons vegetable oil	1 tablespoon melted butter or margarine

Have chicken cut into 10 pieces. Use the giblets, back, neck and wings for broth; add 2 cups water, ½ teaspoon salt, pepper and a small onion. Simmer about 1 hour and strain.

Put flour, salt and pepper into a paper or plastic bag. Shake to combine; toss in chicken pieces to coat with flour. Heat oil in large skillet and brown chicken pieces. Just brown — you are not cooking the chicken.

Meanwhile, preheat oven to 425° F. Put eggs into mixer bowl, and beat thoroughly. Add flour and milk, salt and butter or margarine. Beat so that you have a smooth batter.

Coat a heavy, shallow baking dish, earthenware or iron, of about 3 quart capacity, with shortening and put into oven to heat, about 5 minutes. Quickly pour batter into it, then arrange browned chicken in the batter. Put in oven and bake for 25 minutes. Do not peek! At end of time, turn oven down to 325° F. and bake an additional 15 minutes. Turn off and leave chicken in oven, door ajar, for 5 more minutes. The batter will have risen to come up over the chicken, and you will have a beautiful dish to behold — and eat! A crispy brown crust, with a pudding like interior, super good with gravy.

GRAVY

2 tablespoons all-purpose flour
1 cup light cream or Half and Half

1 cup chicken broth
Salt and pepper

Stir flour into pan drippings and cook for a minute. Stir in cream, then chicken broth. Add salt and pepper as necessary for flavor.

BREAST OF CHICKEN NORMANDY   Yield: 6 servings

4-6 whole broiler-fryer chicken breasts
Salt and pepper
½ teaspoon powdered thyme
½ cup butter, divided
½ pound chicken livers
2 tablespoons finely chopped onions

1 teaspoon salt
1 can (3-4 ounces) chopped
  mushrooms, drained
1 cup (4 ounces) grated Swiss cheese
1 egg, well-beaten
Fine dry bread crumbs

Bone the chicken breasts; place between two pieces of waxed paper and pound to flatten. Sprinkle with salt, pepper and thyme. Prepare stuffing: heat ¼ cup butter in skillet; add chicken livers and onion and sprinkle with salt. Cook slowly until livers are cooked. Remove from heat and stir in mushrooms. Attach food grinder to mixer. Force liver/mushroom mixture through grinder, using largest blade. Stir in grated cheese. Divide stuffing into 4-6 portions and place in center of chicken breasts. Fold sides of breasts over the stuffing and fasten with toothpicks. Roll in beaten egg, then bread crumbs. Chill in refrigerator, uncovered, at least two hours to allow coating to dry. Heat remaining ¼ cup butter in large skillet; add breasts and brown thoroughly on all sides. Put browned chicken breasts in a shallow baking pan and bake at 350° F. for 45 minutes. Pour a little Supreme Sauce over the chicken. Serve remaining sauce separately.

SUPREME SAUCE   Yield: 2½ cups

¼ cup butter
¼ cup all-purpose flour
2 cups chicken stock or canned
  chicken broth

1 tablespoon lemon juice
½ cup light cream

Melt butter in saucepan and blend in flour. Add chicken broth and cook, stirring constantly, until mixture thickens and comes to a boil. Boil gently for 3-5 minutes, stirring constantly. Add lemon juice. Stir in cream. Heat, but do not allow to boil.

LIVER LOAF   Yield: 6-8 servings

1 pound beef liver
1 medium onion, chopped
½ pound pork sausage
1 clove crushed garlic
1 cup dry bread crumbs
1 teaspoon Worcestershire sauce
1 tablespoon lemon juice

1 teaspoon salt
1 teaspoon celery salt
⅛ teaspoon pepper
2 eggs, well beaten
½ cup stock
4 slices bacon

Use a 10 x 5 x 3-inch loaf pan. Cover liver with hot water; simmer 5 minutes. Drain liquid and reserve liquid stock. Preheat oven to 350° F. Put liver and onion through food grinder using vegetable cutter plate. Add remaining ingredients, except bacon. Form into loaf in pan. Top with bacon slices. Bake 45 minutes.

VARIATION:

Place whole hard cooked eggs or whole cooked carrots in the center of the loaf as you form it. It adds a pretty touch of color when you slice the loaf.

SALMON MOUSSE   Yield: 6 servings

1 envelope unflavored gelatin
¼ cup cold water
½ cup boiling water, or liquid drained
    from salmon
1 can (1 pound) salmon
2 teaspoons grated horseradish

1 tablespoon finely minced onion
1 tablespoon lemon juice
⅓ cup finely minced celery
1 cup heavy cream
2 hard cooked eggs, chopped

Soften the gelatin in the cold water; add the boiling water and stir until gelatin is dissolved. Mash the drained salmon in a medium bowl, using a fork; add horse-radish, onion, lemon juice and celery. Using low speed on the mixer, beat in the gelatin mixture. Beat 1-2 minutes, until you obtain a nice smooth creamy mass. Whip cream until stiff and fold into the salmon mixture; fold in eggs. Pour into a 1 quart mold and chill until set. Unmold onto lettuce; garnish with watercress or parsley. Serve as a luncheon dish or on the cocktail table as a spread with breads or crackers.

FISKE PUDDING Yield: 6-8 servings

A Norwegian fish pudding, well worth all the steps involved in making it.

1 pound haddock or other white fish	3 tablespoons all-purpose flour
½ pound (1 cup) butter	1 cup light cream or Half and Half
1 teaspoon salt	1 cup heavy cream, whipped
¼ teaspoon white pepper	Bread crumbs
4 eggs, separated	

Butter and crumb a 1½-quart ring mold or baking dish. Partially fill a deep pan with hot water and place in the oven. The pan should hold the filled baking dish, and the water should come 1½-2-inches up the sides of the dish. Preheat oven to 350° F.

Attach grinder to your mixer, using the meat cutter plate. With fish cut up into thin strips, feed it into the grinder; put ground fish back into grinder and grind again. Add room temperature butter, salt and pepper, and beat thoroughly with your mixer on medium speed. This should result in a very smooth mass. Fold in stiffly beaten egg whites and whipped cream. Pour into mold and cover with greased waxed paper or aluminum foil. Place in the baking pan with boiling water and bake for 1-1½ hours. Allow to sit in pan about 10 minutes, then carefully invert onto serving platter. Garnish with parsley or green peas. Serve with Dilled Hollandaise Sauce.

DILLED HOLLANDAISE SAUCE Yield: 1¼ cups

2 egg yolks	½ cup butter, melted
1½ tablespoons lemon juice	¾ tablespoon chopped fresh dill or
1 teaspoon prepared mustard,	¼ teaspoon dried dill weed
preferably Dijon	½ cup dairy sour cream

In small bowl, combine egg yolks, lemon juice and mustard. Beat at high speed until well blended, then add melted butter, a few drops at a time, beating well after each addition. With a hand beater, stop only very briefly to add the butter.

Serve on vegetables, fish or meat.

HAM QUICHE   Yield: 6-8 servings

Pastry for 9-inch deep pie or
   quiche pan
2 tablespoons butter
1 cup diced cooked ham
1 medium onion, sliced
½ pound mushrooms, sliced
   (optional)

4 ounces grated Swiss cheese
4 eggs
1 cup heavy cream
½ cup milk
¼ teaspoon salt
⅛ teaspoon pepper
⅛ teaspoon nutmeg

Line pie pan with pastry. Preheat oven to 350° F. Sauté ham, onion and mushrooms in butter. Put into pie shell. Top with grated cheese. Beat eggs until frothy; beat in heavy cream, milk and seasonings. Pour into pie shell. Bake 25-30 minutes. Serve warm as an entrée or cold as an appetizer.

GREEN PEPPER, TOMATO & ONION QUICHE   Yield: 6 servings

Pastry for 10-inch pie pan
1 cup (4 ounces) grated Swiss cheese
1 large beefsteak tomato
1 large green pepper
1 medium onion
2 tablespoons butter or margarine

4 large eggs
2 cups light cream
⅛ teaspoon nutmeg
Dash of cayenne pepper
¾ teaspoon salt
¼ teaspoon black pepper

Prepare pie crust and line 10-inch pan. Flute edges and put in refrigerator to chill. Preheat oven to 450° F. Attach shredder attachment to mixer; grate cheese. Set aside. Peel tomato and slice in thick slices. Remove seeds from green pepper and cut pepper into 1-inch squares. Slice onion. Melt butter in large skillet over low heat. Add green pepper and onion and gently sauté for 7-10 minutes. Do not allow to brown.

Arrange tomato slices on bottom of crust. Add pepper and onion, distributing evenly over tomato. Sprinkle cheese over vegetables. In small bowl, beat the eggs thoroughly, and beat in remaining ingredients. Pour over cheese-vegetable mixture and put in preheated oven. Reduce heat to 400° F. and bake 10 minutes; reduce heat to 325° F. and continue to bake until the custard is set, 25-30 minutes.

BACON-CHEESE PUFF   Yield: 8 servings

A wonderful Brunch or Supper dish.

10 slices bacon
2 medium onions, sliced
12 slices firm type white bread,
    cut into fourths
½ pound Swiss cheese, shredded

8 eggs
4 cups milk
1 teaspoon salt
¼ teaspoon pepper

Cook bacon until crisp; drain thoroughly. Cook onion in bacon drippings just until soft. Do not brown. Drain. Cover the bottom of a 9 x 13-inch pan with bread. Crumble the bacon and sprinkle half over the bread, then half the onions, and half the cheese. Repeat. In large mixer bowl, beat the eggs thoroughly, slowly beat in the milk and salt and pepper. Pour this mixture over the layers in the pan. You can now refrigerate this up to 12 hours. Preheat oven to 350° F. and bake 45-50 minutes. This recipe can be cut in half quite easily and baked in an 8 x 8 x 2-inch pan to make 4 servings.

RICOTTA SPINACH PIE   Yield: 6-8 servings

1 (10 ounce) package frozen chopped
    spinach
2 tablespoons butter
⅛ teaspoon black pepper
¾ teaspoon salt
¾ teaspoon dill weed
1 medium onion, chopped

2 tablespoons all-purpose flour
3 eggs
1 pound ricotta cheese
½ cup grated sharp Cheddar cheese
1 9-inch unbaked pastry shell
1 cup sour cream
Paprika

Preheat oven to 375° F. Drain the spinach very thoroughly. Squeeze dry. Sauté gently in the melted butter along with onion, black pepper, salt and dill weed. When onion is translucent, sprinkle with flour. In large mixer bowl beat eggs thoroughly; beat in the ricotta cheese and Cheddar cheese. Spread into pie shell, cover with sour cream and sprinkle with paprika. Bake 45-50 minutes. Delicious hot; good cold.

CHEESE AND WHITE WINE CASSEROLE

Yield: 6 servings

A cheese fondue without the dipping.

6 slices firm type white bread
5 tablespoons butter
1 garlic clove, crushed
6 eggs
½ cup heavy cream

½ cup chicken boullion
¼ teaspoon dry mustard
1 teaspoon paprika
½ pound Gruyere cheese, grated
1½ cups dry white wine

Trim crusts from bread. Cream butter and garlic together and spread on bread. Arrange in casserole buttered side down. Beat eggs until foamy, beat in cream. Add boullion, mustard, paprika, cheese and wine, stirring only enough to mix. Pour over bread. Bake in preheated 350° F. oven for 30 minutes or until puffed and brown. Serve immediately with a crisp green salad.

ZUCCHINI FRITTATA

Yield: 6 servings

1 tablespoon olive oil
3 cups thickly sliced zucchini
½ small onion, finely minced
¼ cup fresh parsley
8 eggs

1 cup (8 ounces) grated cheese
½ teaspoon oregano
½ teaspoon basil
¼ teaspoon salt
⅛ teaspoon black pepper

Preheat oven to 350° F. Grease lightly a 9-inch square pan. Slice zucchini using slicer attachment. Heat oil in large skillet and sauté zucchini, onion and parsley until zucchini is softened, about 5 minutes. Set aside. In large bowl, at medium speed, beat eggs, cheese and seasonings. By hand, stir in zucchini mixture, blending well. Pour into pan and bake until firm in center, 20-25 minutes. Serve hot or cold. NOTE: A good way to use any leftover cheese as well as surplus garden zucchini. For maximum Italian flavor, use Parmesan or Romano cheese, cutting back to ¾ cup.

NOODLE CHEESE PUFF

Yield: 6-8 servings

3 eggs, separated
½ cup melted butter
2 teaspoons granulated sugar
1 pound creamed cottage cheese
  (small curd)

1 cup (8 ounces) sour cream
8 ounces medium noodles, cooked
  and drained
½ cup soft fresh bread crumbs
3 tablespoons melted butter

Preheat oven to 350° F. Butter generously a two-quart casserole. Beat the egg yolks until very light; beat in melted butter and sugar. By hand, stir in cottage cheese, sour cream and drained noodles. Beat egg whites until stiff and fold into cheese mixture. Pour into prepared casserole. Toss bread crumbs into the 3 tablespoons melted butter; sprinkle over top of casserole. Bake 45-50 minutes.

CHEESE SOUFFLE   Yield: 4 servings

¼ cup butter
¼ cup all-purpose flour
1 cup milk
1½ cups (6 ounces) grated Cheddar or
   Swiss cheese
¼ cup grated Parmesan cheese

¾ teaspoon salt
Dash of black pepper
⅛ teaspoon nutmeg
6 egg yolks
8 egg whites

Preheat oven to 375° F. Generously grease 1½-quart casserole or soufflé dish which has a waxed paper collar attached. Grease the waxed paper also. Melt butter, stir in flour. Add milk gradually and cook over low heat, stirring constantly until mixture comes to a boil. Remove from heat and stir in cheese until it melts. Add salt, pepper and nutmeg. Beat egg yolks and add to the mixture. Wash beaters thoroughly. Beat egg whites until stiff but not dry. Fold into egg-cheese mixture. Pour into prepared baking dish and bake 35-40 minutes. Serve at once. This can be prepared ahead up to the addition of the egg whites. Once the egg whites have been folded in, the soufflé has to be baked, then served immediately.

SPINACH CHEESE SOUFFLE   Yield: 4 servings

1 (10 ounce) package frozen chopped
   spinach, cooked
3 tablespoons butter
4 tablespoons all-purpose flour
½ teaspoon salt

Dash of black pepper
⅛ teaspoon nutmeg
1 cup light cream
1½ cups grated Swiss cheese
3 eggs, separated

Butter a 1½-quart casserole or soufflé dish. Preheat oven to 325° F. Drain cooked spinach thoroughly; squeeze dry and leave in colander. Melt butter, blend in flour, cook 1 minute. Add seasonings; slowly stir in cream, cooking until smooth. Add cheese, stir to blend. Beat egg yolks until thick; combine with spinach and sauce. Beat egg whites until stiff and fold into spinach mixture. Pour into prepared pan and bake 45-50 minutes, until puffed and lightly browned. Serve at once.

CALZONE
Yield: 1 10-inch roll; 6 servings

An Italian treat.

Dough

2¾-3¼ cups all-purpose flour
1 tablespoon granulated sugar
1 teaspoon salt

1 package active dry yeast
1 cup warm water
2 tablespoons vegetable oil

Filling

½ cup chopped green pepper
½ cup chopped onion
1 tablespoon olive oil
½ teaspoon salt
¼ teaspoon pepper
1 pound ricotta cheese

½ pound grated mozzarella cheese
½ cup grated Romano or Parmesan cheese
½ pound prosciuto or Italian Hot ham
3 tablespoons melted butter

Mix 1 cup flour, the sugar, salt and the yeast in a large bowl. Add warm water and 2 tablespoons oil. Beat at medium speed 2-3 minutes, or until smooth. If using stand mixer, insert dough hooks and add enough remaining flour to make a smooth elastic dough, kneading about 4-5 minutes at low speed. If not kneading with a mixer, turn dough onto lightly floured surface; knead until smooth and elastic, about 8 minutes. Place in greased bowl; turn greased side up. Cover; let rise in warm place until double, about 1 hour.

Sauté the green pepper and onion in the olive oil until tender. Add salt and pepper and when done, drain thoroughly. Combine with the cheeses; cut up the ham and add to the mixture.

Preheat oven to 375° F. After dough has doubled in volume, punch down and roll out into a very thin rectangle, about 28 x 10-inches. Spread cheese mixture across the center third of the rectangle; fold one side over the cheese and spread with melted butter; fold other side over and spread remaining butter on entire roll. Pinch the ends together so filling does not bubble out. Bake for 30 minutes or until nicely browned. If desired, brush with melted butter once more. Allow to cool slightly before slicing.

Pizzas:

Note: This amount of dough will also make two 12-inch pizzas. Grease two 12-inch pizza pans. Divide dough into two balls; press out the dough to fit each pan. Spread with your favorite tomato sauce, cheeses, or whatever toppings you like best. Bake 25 minutes in a preheated 400° F. oven.

SPINACH PIE   Yield: 10-12 servings

Spanakopita

3 (10 ounce) packages frozen
  chopped spinach
1 pound feta cheese, crumbled
6 eggs, separated
4 chopped green onions

½ pound melted butter
¼ teaspoon pepper
½ pound phyllo pastry sheets
  (12-15 sheets)

Optional: You can add ½ cup chopped parsley or mint leaves to the filling.

Drain uncooked thawed spinach in colander for several hours, squeezing dry. Place in a bowl; add cheese, chopped onion and pepper and mix thoroughly. Stir in egg yolks, which have been slightly beaten. Beat egg whites stiff and fold into spinach mixture.

To assemble: Grease 13 x 9 x 2-inch pan, using melted butter. Place pastry sheet in the pan and brush liberally with butter. Continue doing this until you have 6 layers of pastry. (Be sure to keep opened package of phyllo covered with damp cloth to keep it from drying out.) Be generous with the butter, being certain to brush each layer. Spread spinach mixture evenly over the pastry layers. Cover with 6 more individually buttered pastry sheets. Bake in a 350° F. oven 40-45 minutes or until golden brown. Cut into squares. Serve hot.

Hint: Don't cut the phyllo dough to fit the pan — you don't want to waste it. Just tuck it down into the sides of the pan. It's all quite good and will make the pie better!

EGGROLLS   Yield: 15-20 eggrolls

1 cup shredded celery
2 medium onions, shredded
¾ pound regular cabbage, shredded
¼ pound beef or pork
½ teaspoon dry sherry
½ teaspoon cornstarch
⅛ teaspoon pepper

2 teaspoons soy sauce
¼ teaspoon granulated sugar
1½ teaspoons salt
2 medium slices ginger root
½ pound fresh bean sprouts
Cooking oil for deep frying
2 packages eggroll skins

Attach shredder to electric mixer; shred celery, onions and cabbage.

Marinate the meat with the dry sherry, cornstarch, pepper, soy sauce and sugar for at least half an hour.

Put a small amount of oil in a wok or skillet over medium heat. Add salt and the ginger. Then add the shredded onions and celery and cook about three minutes or until half cooked. Add the meat, stirring constantly to keep the meat in tiny pieces. When cooked, place mixture in a colander, straining liquid into a bowl. Spread mixture out on a plate and allow to cool. Discard ginger.

Put the drained liquid in the wok or skillet; stir-fry the cabbage in the liquid until the cabbage is cooked. Cool. Rinse the bean sprouts and add to the cabbage, then mix in the meat mixture. The sprouts should be added at the last minute or they will become limp.

Place a large spoonful of filling on the eggroll skin, just below the center. Fold up one point of the rectangle, then fold over both sides, then fold down the top triangle and wet edges with water to seal. Deep fry at 350-400° F. until golden brown on all sides. Drain on paper towels. Serve with Plum Sauce.

QUICHE LORRAINE   Yield: 6-8 as a main dish/8-10 as first course

1 10-inch unbaked pie shell
1 cup grated Swiss cheese
10 slices bacon
4 eggs
2 cups light cream

¼ teaspoon granulated sugar
⅛ teaspoon nutmeg
Dash of cayenne pepper
¾ teaspoon salt
¼ teaspoon black pepper

Refrigerate pie shell while making filling. Preheat oven to 450° F. Fry bacon crisp; drain and crumble. Set aside with grated cheese. Put eggs in mixing bowl and beat; add remaining ingredients and beat together until thoroughly combined. Sprinkle cheese and bacon over pie shell; pour egg mixture over all. Put the quiche in the preheated oven; reduce heat to 400° F. and bake 11 minutes. Reduce heat to 325° F. and bake until set and lightly browned, about 25-30 minutes.

CHEESE STRATA
Yield: 6 servings

6 slices firm type bread
Butter or margarine
1 cup shredded sharp cheese
1½ cups milk
1 teaspoon salt

⅛ teaspoon cayenne pepper or
    several dashes red pepper
    seasoning
3 eggs

Butter the bread then cut into ½-inch cubes. Arrange in a 1½-quart baking dish in alternate layers with the cheese. Beat eggs thoroughly. Beat in the milk and seasonings. Pour over bread and cheese. Let stand at least 30 minutes, or refrigerate overnight. Bake in preheated 350° F. oven 30-35 minutes or until brown and puffy.

GARDEN VEGETABLE TART
Yield: 8 servings

1 10-inch unbaked pie shell
¼ pound fresh mushrooms, diced
1 small zucchini squash, diced
2 tablespoons butter or margarine
1 pound ricotta cheese
1 cup grated mozzarella cheese
3 large eggs

½ cup cooked spinach, squeezed dry
1 tablespoon melted butter or
    margarine
1 tablespoon dried dill weed
1 teaspoon garlic salt
½ teaspoon pepper

Line a large 9-inch pan with pastry. Refrigerate while making filling. Preheat oven to 350° F. Sauté mushrooms and zucchini in butter or margarine until almost cooked. In large bowl, beat the eggs thoroughly; beat in remaining ingredients. By hand, stir in vegetable mixture. Fill quiche shell. Bake 35-40 minutes or until knife inserted in center comes out clean. Can be served hot or cold.

PIROSHKI Yield: 8-10 servings

Russian in origin — an economical meal.

1 package active dry yeast	½ teaspoon salt
¼ cup warm water (110-115° F.)	1¼-2 cups all-purpose flour
¾ cup warm milk	Filling
1 tablespoon granulated sugar	

Insert dough hooks. Dissolve yeast in warm water in medium bowl. At low speed, stir in milk, sugar, salt and ½ cup flour. Beat at medium speed one minute. At low speed, add enough more flour for a smooth dough, kneading 5 minutes. Place in a greased bowl and roll the ball to grease the dough. Let rise in warm place until double, about 45 minutes. Punch down. Roll dough out on lightly floured board till very thin, about 1/16-inch. Cut into 5-inch circles, rerolling scraps. Place ¼ cup filling on each circle; bring ends together to seal and shape Piroshki so that they are thick in the middle and taper at both ends. Place seam side down on greased baking sheets. Cover and let rise until puffy, 40-45 minutes. Preheat oven to 375° F. Bake until golden brown, 18-20 minutes. Serve hot with sour cream, if desired.

FILLING:

1 medium onion, finely chopped	½ teaspoon salt
1 clove garlic, crushed	⅛ teaspoon pepper
1 tablespoon butter or margarine	1 teaspoon dried dill weed
¾ pound lean ground beef, lamb or chicken	1 hard-cooked egg, finely chopped

Cook onion and garlic in butter until tender, but not browned. Stir in meat and cook until brown. Add remaining ingredients.

Note: Beside using raw ground meat, you can grind up leftover cooked meat of just about any kind and use to fill Piroshki.

Chapter Six
GARDEN VARIETY GOODNESS

BROCCOLI SOUFFLE   Yield: 6-8 servings

½ pounds broccoli, washed and
   and cut (1 large bunch)
3 tablespoons butter or margarine
1 garlic clove
5 tablespoons all-purpose flour
1 cup heavy cream

1 teaspoon salt
¼ teaspoon pepper
¼ teaspoon nutmeg
4 eggs, separated
2 ounces (½ cup) grated Parmesan
   cheese

Thoroughly grease a 6-cup ring mold, then coat with flour, knocking out excess. Wash broccoli and cut up. Cook until just tender in a small amount of boiling, salted water, approximately 12 minutes. Chop fine.

Preheat oven to 350° F. Melt butter. Crush garlic and sauté gently in the butter, to release the flavor. Do not brown. Add the flour and cook gently for 1 minute, stirring constantly. Do not allow to turn brown. Add cream; when thickened, add broccoli and remove from heat. Add salt, pepper and nutmeg, stir in slightly beaten egg yolks. On high speed, beat the egg whites until stiff peaks form; fold into broccoli mixture along with grated Parmesan cheese. Pour into mold.

Stand mold in a pan containing enough boiling water to come up 1-inch on the sides of the mold. Bake 35-40 minutes or until nicely browned and puffed up. Loosen sides of soufflé with a knife and invert onto a large plate. Fill center with glazed sliced carrots or tiny new potatoes.

CARROT MOLD   Yield: 6 servings

1½ cups shredded carrot, 2 medium
1 cup all-purpose flour
½ teaspoon baking powder
½ teaspoon salt

½ cup margarine, softened
¾ cup brown sugar
1 egg

Preheat oven to 350° F. Grease a 5½-cup ring mold. Shred carrots using finest blade of your mixer shredder attachment. Stir together flour, baking powder and salt. In large mixing bowl, cream shortening and sugar; beat in the egg. Stir in flour mixture until completely combined, then add carrots. Pour into prepared pan and bake 45 minutes. To serve, fill the center with green peas, or other dark green vegetables.

ZUCCHINI AND RICE   Yield: 6 servings

2 tablespoons olive oil
1 onion, finely chopped
2 garlic cloves, minced
1 cup brown rice
2 cups beef or chicken broth
½ teaspoon ground rosemary
¾ cup chopped parsley

½ teaspoon salt
1½ pounds zucchini
½ cup grated Cheddar cheese
2 tablespoons olive oil
1 garlic clove, minced
¾ cup sliced ripe olives, optional

Heat the oil in a saucepan and add onion and garlic. Sauté lightly and add rice. Cook until rice starts to change color. Add 1 cup of the chicken or beef broth; cover and simmer over low heat. When broth is absorbed, add the other cup of broth and continue to cook over low heat. Add rosemary, parsley and salt. Attach slicer attachment to mixer and slice zucchini using the thickest slicer. Attach shredder blade and shred the cheese. Set aside. Heat the second amount of oil in a skillet and sauté the zucchini and chopped garlic. When rice is done, stir in the cooked zucchini and the grated cheese, stirring until the cheese melts. Add the sliced olives if desired.

SWEET AND SOUR CABBAGE   Yield: 6 servings

1 large head red cabbage
2 apples
¼ cup butter
2 tablespoons finely chopped onion

¼ cup hot water
2 teaspoons salt
¼ cup dry red wine
¼ cup light brown sugar

Cut cabbage into sections and remove core. Shred, using mixer attachment. Core the apples, but do not peel. Cut into thin slices.

In a saucepan, melt butter and sauté onion for a few minutes. Add cabbage, cover and simmer for 15 minutes. Add apple slices, water and salt; stir. Cover and simmer about 20 minutes, or until tender. Water should be absorbed. Add wine and brown sugar and simmer 10-15 more minutes. Serve hot.

TWICE BAKED POTATOES
Yield: 6 servings

6 baking potatoes
3 tablespoons butter or margarine
½ cup sour cream
1 egg
1 tablespoon finely minced green
   onion or chives

1 cup grated Cheddar cheese
½ teaspoon salt
¼ teaspoon freshly ground pepper
Grated Parmesan cheese

Bake the potatoes at 375° F. for 1 hour or until done.

Cut tops from potatoes, and carefully remove inside of potatoes from skins, to the large mixer bowl. Add butter or margarine, sour cream and egg; beat at medium speed until fluffy. At low speed, stir in onion, cheese, salt and pepper.

Use to fill potato skins or, if desired, fill individual tins or a casserole. Sprinkle with grated Parmesan cheese. Bake at 350° F. 20-30 minutes or until top is browned and potatoes are heated through.

SPINACH PUFF
Yield: 3-4 servings

1 (10 ounce) package frozen chopped
   spinach
1 (8 ounce) jar processed cheese
   spread

1 tablespoon all-purpose flour
2 eggs, separated

Preheat oven to 350° F. Grease thoroughly a 3-4 cup baking dish. Cook spinach; drain thoroughly, squeezing dry. Heat cheese spread over low heat. Remove from heat; blend in flour and egg yolks. Stir in spinach. Beat egg whites until stiff; fold into the cheese-spinach mixture. Pour into baking dish. Bake 30 minutes.

SOUR CREAM POTATO SALAD
Yield: 6-8 servings

6 medium potatoes
1 small onion, minced
1½ teaspoons salt
4 tablespoons granulated sugar
¼ teaspoon black pepper

3 hard-cooked eggs
1 cup sour cream
2 tablespoons cider vinegar
½ teaspoon dry mustard
6 slices lean bacon, cooked

Cook potatoes in skins; when cool enough to handle, peel. Slice crosswise into thin slices and put into a large bowl. Add onion. Sprinkle with salt, sugar, pepper; stir in 1 sliced hard-cooked egg. In small mixing bowl, beat sour cream, vinegar and mustard until very light and fluffy. Pour over potatoes; stir in very lightly. Garnish salad with sliced egg and sprinkle with bacon. Serve in lettuce bowls.

FAVORITE COLE SLAW

Yield: 6-8 servings

1 large head cabbage
3 tablespoons finely chopped green
  onion

1 green pepper, finely chopped
2 carrots (optional)

DRESSING

½ cup mayonnaise
½ cup sour cream
3-4 tablespoons red wine vinegar

1 teaspoon salt
¼ teaspoon pepper
¼ cup granulated sugar
  (more if you like)

Using the slicer attachment on your mixer, finely slice the head of cabbage. If using the carrots, shred them on the fine blade. Combine vegetables in large bowl. In small bowl, beat together at low speed the ingredients for the dressing and pour over the cabbage; toss until well combined. Chill at least several hours. This will keep one or two days if refrigerated and tightly covered with plastic wrap. Be sure to stir thoroughly before serving.

MOLDED BANANA SALAD

Yield: 6-8 servings

1 (3 ounce) package strawberry
  gelatin
1 cup hot water
2 bananas, mashed
1 small can (8 ounce) crushed
  pineapple

1 small package (10 ounces) frozen
  sliced strawberries, thawed
1 (3 ounce) package cream cheese
1 cup sour cream

Use a 1½-quart mold. Dissolve gelatin in hot water; chill until it starts to thicken. Add mashed bananas, pineapple and strawberries. Pour half into the mold and chill until firm. In small mixer bowl, beat together until fluffy the cream cheese and sour cream. Spread over top of layer in mold; chill. Pour remaining gelatin mixture over top.

CRANBERRY JELLY SALAD MOLD   Yield: 10-12 servings

3 (3 ounce) packages raspberry gelatin
3 cups water (use pineapple juice to
   make up 3 cups)
1 can crushed pineapple, thoroughly
   drained (any size)

1 pint sour cream
1 can (16 ounces) whole cranberry
   sauce
Chopped walnuts or other nuts, if
   desired

Dissolve gelatin in hot water and allow to set until it begins to thicken. Put into large bowl and beat at medium speed, gradually beating in the sour cream until smooth. Stir in the cranberry sauce, crushed pineapple and nuts. Pour into mold and refrigerate until set.

CUCUMBER CREAM SALAD   Yield: 8 servings

1 (3 ounce) package lime gelatin
¾ teaspoon salt
1 cup hot water
2 tablespoons white vinegar
1 teaspoon grated onion

½ cup mayonnaise
1 cup sour cream, chilled thoroughly
2 cups seeded, finely chopped peeled
   cucumbers, thoroughly drained

Dissolve gelatin and salt in hot water; stir in vinegar and onion. Chill until slightly thickened. Stir in mayonnaise, blending thoroughly. In small bowl whip the chilled sour cream until it is light and fluffy, and fold into the gelatin mixture. Fold in cucumber. Pour into 8 individual molds; chill until firm. Unmold on greens.

Note: Can be molded in a loaf pan. Unmold onto greens on large serving platter. Garnish with carrot curls and radish roses.

RAW VEGETABLES IN SOUR CREAM   Yield: 4 cups, 6-8 servings

2 cups sliced radishes
2 cups sliced cucumbers
½ cup minced scallions

2 teaspoons salt
1 teaspoon granulated sugar
1 cup sour cream

Attach slicer to mixer; slice radishes using thinnest slicer; slice cucumbers with thicker slicer blade. Chill thoroughly. Mix salt, sugar and sour cream and minced scallions and sliced vegetables. Serve in chilled bowls.

BREAD AND BUTTER PICKLES   Yield: 6 pints

3 quarts sliced cucumbers
(about 20 small)
4 large onions, sliced

3 peppers (use 1 red for color), cut into
thin rings

Use slicer attachment on mixer. Combine vegetables, sprinkle with ⅓ cup salt (not iodized), and let stand for 3 hours. Cover liberally with ice cubes. At the end of 3 hours, put all in a colander and drain thoroughly.

1 quart cider vinegar
3 cups granulated sugar (use more if
you desire a sweeter pickle)
1 teaspoon mustard seed

1 teaspoon whole cloves
1 teaspoon celery seed
1 teaspoon turmeric

Combine in a large kettle and heat. Add cucumbers and bring to the boiling point. DO NOT BOIL. Fill hot sterilized pint jars and seal immediately.

SUMMER SQUASH PICKLES   Yield: 4 pints

A pretty and tasty addition to the relish tray.

8 cups summer squash, sliced
2½ cups onion, sliced
1 cup green pepper, diced
1 tablespoon salt (not iodized)

2 cups cider vinegar
3 cups granulated sugar
1½ teaspoons mustard seed
1 teaspoon celery seed

Use the slicer attachment on your mixer. Cut squash and onions into thin slices. You may have to cut them in half to feed them through. Combine them with salt, mix well. Allow to stand for 3 hours. Drain very thoroughly. Combine remaining ingredients in a large saucepan. Stir to dissolve sugar, then allow to come to a full, rolling boil. Meanwhile, pack pepper, squash and onions in hot sterilized jars. Pour in the pickling solution to within ¼-inch of the top. Seal jars and process in a boiling water bath for 15 minutes.

ZUCCHINI RELISH   Yield: 6 pints

12 cups sliced zucchini
4 cups sliced onions
1 red pepper
1 green pepper
5 tablespoons salt (not iodized)
2½ cups cider vinegar
6 cups granulated sugar

1 tablespoon dry mustard
¾ teaspoon nutmeg
¾ teaspoon turmeric
1 tablespoon cornstarch
1½ teaspoons celery seed
½ teaspoon black pepper

Slice zucchini and onions using the mixer slicer attachment. Measure after slicing; cut up into smaller pieces. Attach the grinder, using the coarse chopping blade. Chop zucchini, onions, red and green peppers. Mix in the salt and allow to stand overnight. Rinse with cold water and drain thoroughly in colander.

Using a large pot, mix together remaining ingredients; bring to a boil and cook for a few minutes to thicken slightly. Add drained ground vegetables and mix thoroughly. Bring to a boil, lower heat and simmer for 30 minutes. Fill hot sterilized jars and seal. Store in cool, dark place.

COPLEY PLAZA RELISH   Yield: 3 pints

A very mild relish, with no spices.

1 quart (1¾ pounds) chopped green
    tomatoes
1 quart (1¾ pounds) chopped ripe
    tomatoes
5 small onions, peeled and chopped

½ cup salt (not iodized)
3 sweet red peppers, chopped
2 sweet green peppers, chopped
2 cups white vinegar
2 cups granulated sugar

Put tomatoes and onions through food grinder, using coarse blade; sprinkle with salt and let stand 12 hours. Drain well in a colander, pressing out all the salt brine. Grind peppers and add along with vinegar and sugar, and cook together about 30 minutes. Place in hot, sterilized jars and seal at once.

Delicious with baked beans, corned beef, baked and broiled fish as well as fish cakes, or combined with French dressing for salads.

CHILI SAUCE   Yield: 2-3 (8 ounce) jars

12 large red tomatoes, peeled
2 green peppers
2 onions
1 cup cider vinegar

1¼ cup granulated sugar
1 tablespoon salt
½ teaspoon ground cloves
2½ teaspoons cinnamon

To peel tomatoes quickly, boil about a quart of water. Plunge tomatoes in water for a few seconds, or just long enough to loosen skins. The skin should lift right off.

Grind vegetables using the coarse blade of the grinder attachment. Add vinegar, sugar, salt and spices. Simmer about 3 hours, pour into hot sterilized jars and seal immediately. This is best if aged several months.

RED PEPPER JAM   Yield: 4 (8 ounce) jars
A beautiful presentation.

1 dozen large sweet red peppers
1 tablespoon salt (not iodized)

1½ cups cider vinegar
3 cups granulated sugar

Remove seeds from peppers and grind, using the finest blade of the grinder attachment. Mix in the salt and let stand three hours. Drain thoroughly. Add vinegar and sugar and simmer slowly until it thickens to the consistency of jam — about 1 hour. Pour into hot sterilized jars and seal. This adds a bright touch of color wherever used. Spread plain cream cheese on cocktail bread or crackers and top with a bit of this jam for a good appetizer.

PEAR-GINGER JAM   Yield: 12 (8 ounce) glasses
Spoon onto breakfast toast or vanilla ice cream!

¼ pound candied ginger
3 pounds ripe pears

7½ cups granulated sugar
1 bottle liquid pectin

Prepare jelly glasses by sterilizing; have jars and covers ready. Dice the ginger into very fine pieces. Put into a large saucepan. Peel and core the pears; attach grinder to mixer and grind the pears using the finest blade. Measure 4 cups of the pears into saucepan with ginger. Add the sugar and mix well. Place over high heat and bring to full rolling boil; boil hard 1 minute, stirring constantly. Remove from heat and at once stir in the bottle of liquid pectin. Stir and skim the jam for 5 minutes to cool slightly and prevent floating fruit. Ladle into prepared glasses and cover as recommended by the jar manufacturer. The jam may set slowly; allow a week or longer.

SALAD DRESSINGS

BASIC MAYONNAISE   Yield: 2½ cups

2 cups vegetable oil, divided
2 egg yolks
1 tablespoon confectioners' sugar
1 teaspoon dry mustard
1 teaspoon salt

¼ teaspoon paprika
Dash of cayenne pepper
2 tablespoons lemon juice, divided
2 tablespoons white vinegar
1 tablespoon hot water (160-180° F.)

Chill vegetable oil, mixing bowl and beaters. Add egg yolks to chilled mixing bowl and beat on high speed for 1 minute. Stop mixer. Add confectioners' sugar, dry mustard, salt, paprika, cayenne pepper and 1 tablespoon lemon juice. Beat on medium speed until well blended, about ½ minute. Scrape sides of bowl as needed. Add ¼ cup oil, drop by drop until mixture thickens. Slowly pour in remaining 1¾ cup oil, alternating with remaining lemon juice and vinegar. When mixture is well blended, add hot water and continue beating until mixture is smooth and creamy. Scrape side of bowl as necessary. Place in a covered jar and chill in refrigerator before using.

BLUE CHEESY DRESSING   Yield: 1 quart

1 cup Basic Mayonnaise
1 cup sour cream
1 cup buttermilk
4-6 ounces blue cheese, crumbled
1 small onion, chopped
1 clove garlic, minced
2 tablespoons lemon juice

2 teaspoons monosodium glutamate
2 teaspoons Worcestershire sauce
¼ teaspoon salt
¼ teaspoon dry mustard
2 drops hot pepper sauce
Dash pepper

Combine all ingredients in a large mixing bowl. Blend on low speed until thoroughly combined.

THOUSAND ISLAND DRESSING   Yield: 2 cups

1 cup Basic Mayonnaise
¼ cup catsup
¼ cup sweet pickle relish
2 tablespoons green pepper, finely
    chopped

2 tablespoons celery, finely chopped
1 tablespoon onion, grated
1 hard-cooked egg, chopped
Dash hot pepper sauce

Combine all ingredients in small mixing bowl. Blend on low speed until thoroughly combined.

LO-CAL DRESSING   Yield: 1½ cups

½ cup catsup
⅓ cup lemon juice
¼ cup salad oil
1 tablespoon onion, grated
1 tablespoon green pepper, chopped
1 tablespoon celery, chopped

1 hard-cooked egg, chopped
1 teaspoon granulated sugar
1 teaspoon prepared mustard
½ teaspoon salt
¼ teaspoon celery seed

Combine all ingredients in a small mixing bowl. Blend on low speed until thoroughly combined.

RUSSIAN DRESSING   Yield: 2 cups

1¼ cups Basic Mayonnaise
⅓ cup chili sauce
1 tablespoon white vinegar
1 tablespoon fresh parsley, chopped
1 green onion, minced

1 teaspoon Worcestershire sauce
1 teaspoon prepared mustard
1 teaspoon prepared horseradish
Dash cayenne pepper

Combine all ingredients in small mixing bowl. Blend on low speed until thoroughly combined.

OLD-FASHIONED SALAD DRESSING   Yield: 2½ cups

1 teaspoon salt
1 teaspoon dry mustard
1 teaspoon powdered onion
4 teaspoons all-purpose flour
4 tablespoons granulated sugar
2 large eggs

⅔ cup cider vinegar
1 cup light cream
1 tablespoon softened butter or
    margarine
Salt, pepper

Combine first five ingredients in large mixer bowl. Add eggs. Beat on medium speed until completely blended. Turn mixer to low speed; beat in vinegar then cream. Transfer to heavy saucepan and cook on low heat, stirring constantly until thickened. Remove from heat and stir in butter. Season to taste with salt, pepper. Refrigerate.

Serving suggestion: Good served hot as sauce for cooked, sliced potatoes or sliced hard-cooked eggs.

FLUFFY CUCUMBER DRESSING   Yield: 2½ cups

Serve over lettuce wedges.

1 cup heavy cream
½ teaspoon salt
¼ teaspoon paprika
3 tablespoons lemon juice

¼ cup mayonnaise
1 cup chopped cucumber, pared,
   seeded and drained

Whip cream until stiff in small mixer bowl, using recommended speed. Add salt and paprika while whipping. When stiff, turn to low speed and stir in lemon juice and mayonnaise. Turn off mixer and, by hand, stir in cucumber. Serve at once.

WHIPPED CREAM DRESSING   Yield: 1¾ cups

¼ cup honey
1 cup mayonnaise or salad dressing
½ cup heavy cream, whipped stiff

At low speed, beat honey into mayonnaise, then fold in heavy cream. Serve over fruit salad.

CREAMY FRUIT DRESSING   Yield: 1½ cups

1 (3 ounce) package cream cheese
1 tablespoon lemon juice

3 tablespoons currant jelly
¾ cup heavy cream, whipped

Combine at medium speed the cream cheese, lemon juice and currant jelly. When smooth and creamy, add the heavy whipped cream. Serve over fruit.

Chapter Seven
DESSERTS AND OTHER DELICACIES

BASIC BAVARIAN   Yield: Makes about 4 cups, or 6-8 servings

1 package (3 ounces) gelatin
  (any fruit flavor)
⅓ cup granulated sugar
1 tablespoon lemon juice

1 cup boiling water
½ cup cold water or fruit juice
1 envelope whipped topping mix

Dissolve gelatin and sugar in boiling water. Add lemon juice and cold water or fruit juice. Chill for approximately 45 minutes or until soft gel stage. Prepare topping mix as directed on package in large mixing bowl on high speed. Add slightly thickened gelatin mixture to whipped topping and thoroughly blend on medium speed. Pour into a 1½-quart mold or bowl or 8-10 individual molds or serving dishes. Chill until firm, or freeze until firm, about 4 hours. To serve, unmold and garnish with sliced fresh fruit, drained canned fruit, and/or whipped cream.

Note: If desired, 1 cup sliced or diced fresh or drained canned or frozen fruit may be folded into Bavarian before molding. The drained fruit syrup may be used in the gelatin.

BAKED CUSTARD   Yield: 6-8 servings

4 eggs or 6 yolks
⅓ granulated sugar
¼ teaspoon salt

3 cups milk or Half and Half
1½ teaspoons vanilla extract
Nutmeg

Preheat oven to 300° F. Beat eggs on high speed for ½ minute. Add sugar and salt to eggs. Continue beating on high speed for ½ minute. Stir in milk and vanilla on low speed for 1 minute. Pour custard into buttered custard cups. Sprinkle with nutmeg. Set cups or casserole in shallow pan. Add water, enough for ½-inch depth. Bake at 300° F. (slow oven) 1 hour or until knife inserted in center comes out clean.

LEMON SPONGE PUDDING   Yield: 4 servings

2 eggs, separated
2 tablespoons butter
1 cup granulated sugar

3 tablespoons all-purpose flour
4 tablespoons lemon juice
1 cup milk

Preheat oven to 350° F. Grease a 1-quart casserole or baking dish. Beat egg whites until stiff; set aside. At medium speed, cream butter and sugar until light; add egg yolks, one at a time and beat well. At low speed, blend in flour, lemon juice, then milk. Fold in the beaten egg whites. Pour into prepared baking pan; place baking pan in larger pan of cold water. Bake about 45 minutes or until browned on top.

Note: This pudding should come out in two layers — a cake-like top and a lemon sauce on the bottom.

CRANBERRY MELT-AWAY   Yield: 6 servings

1½ cups cranberries
¼ cup brown sugar
¼ cup chopped walnuts
1 egg
¼ cup granulated sugar

½ cup sifted all-purpose flour
⅓ cup butter or margarine, melted
   and cooled
Vanilla ice cream

Preheat oven to 375° F. Spread cranberries on bottom of buttered 9-inch pie plate. Sprinkle with brown sugar and nuts. Beat egg in small bowl until very thick; gradually add sugar, beating until well blended. At low speed, add flour and melted butter or margarine. Beat well at medium speed. Pour batter over cranberries. Bake for 45 minutes. Cut into wedges; serve warm with ice cream.

CREPES POLYNESIAN   Yield: 3½ cups

1 cup heavy cream
2 tablespoons confectioners' sugar
½ teaspoon vanilla extract
1 (16 ounce) can pineapple chunks,
   drained

1 (11 ounce) can mandarin oranges,
   drained
1 banana
1 teaspoon rum
½ cup coconut, toasted

In large mixing bowl whip cream on high speed. Add sugar and vanilla and continue beating until cream is thickened. Reserve ⅓ for topping. Gently mix fruit with rum and coconut. Fold fruit mixture into whipped cream. Spoon filling onto crêpe and fold. Top with whipped cream.

Suggested Crêpe Batter: Basic dessert

CHEESE BLINTZES   Yield: 1 to 1½ cups filling

1 cup ricotta cheese
⅔ cup cottage cheese
¼ cup confectioners' sugar

½ teaspoon vanilla extract
½ teaspoon grated lemon peel
Strawberry preserves

Combine all ingredients in small mixing bowl on medium speed. Spoon onto crêpe. Fold and place in greased 8 x 6 x 2-inch baking dish. Keep warm in moderate oven. To serve spread with melted butter and sprinkle with confectioners' sugar. Top with strawberry preserves.

Suggested Crêpe Batter: Basic dessert

FRENCH SILK CREPE   Yield: 8 servings

½ cup butter, softened
¾ cup confectioners' sugar
2 ounces unsweetened chocolate,
    melted and cooled

1 teaspoon vanilla extract
2 eggs
Sweetened whipped cream
Shaved chocolate

In small mixing bowl cream butter on high speed. Turn to medium speed. Add sugar, blend, gradually increasing speed until mixture becomes light and fluffy. Add chocolate, vanilla and 1 egg. Beat on high speed for 1 minute. Add second egg. Beat 1 minute longer. Chill for 2 hours. Spoon onto crêpe. Fold. Garnish with whipped cream and shaved chocolate

Suggested Crêpe Batter: Basic dessert

BASIC DESSERT CREPES   Yield: 12-14 crêpes

4 eggs
½ cup milk
½ cup water
½ teaspoon salt
2 tablespoons melted margarine or
    butter

2 teaspoons granulated sugar
1 teaspoon vanilla extract
1 cup all-purpose flour

Measure all ingredients except flour into large mixing bowl. Beat on medium speed gradually adding flour, until all ingredients are combined. If small lumps are present, pour through strainer. Pour batter into an 8 or 9-inch lightly greased fry pan. Fry until edges turn light brown and batter no longer steams. Gently loosen edges. Remove from pan and stack on a plate.

VARIATION:

CHOCOLATE CREPES

Add 2 tablespoons chocolate sauce to above recipe.

LEMON DELIGHT   Yield: 9 servings

1 (3 ounce) package lemon gelatin
½ cup granulated sugar
3 tablespoons lemon juice
2 tablespoons grated lemon rind
1 cup boiling water

1 (13 ounce) can evaporated milk,
    chilled
5 (2 x 2-inch) Graham Cracker
    Squares
Maraschino cherries

Dissolve lemon gelatin and sugar in large mixing bowl with 1 cup boiling water. Add lemon juice and grated lemon rind and stir until thoroughly blended. Chill for approximately 45 minutes or until soft gel stage. While gelatin is cooling, crush graham crackers into fine crumbs in a blender, food processor or by mashing on a flat surface with rolling pin. Place partially set gelatin mixture in large mixing bowl on mixer turntable. Beat on high speed while gradually adding evaporated milk. Continue beating for another 1 to 2 minutes until mixture is thick and fluffy. Pour mixture into an 8 x 8 x 2-inch pan. Spread graham cracker crumbs over top and decorate with Maraschino cherries. Chill for several hours. Cut into squares and serve.

CREAMY PINEAPPLE-CHEESE DESSERT   Yield: 12-16 servings

Crumb crust
1 can (20 ounces) crushed pineapple
1 (6 ounce) package pineapple or
    lemon gelatin
2 cups boiling water
1 package (8 ounce) cream cheese,
    softened

½ teaspoon grated orange or lemon
    rind
¼ cup granulated sugar
1½ teaspoons vanilla extract
2 cups sour cream

Prepare crumb crust and press into 9-inch square pan. Drain pineapple, reserving syrup. Dissolve gelatin in boiling water. Add syrup; cool slightly. Combine ½ cup gelatin and the crushed pineapple. Set aside. In a large bowl blend cream cheese, orange rind, sugar and vanilla on medium speed. Turn to low speed and gradually blend remaining gelatin into cheese mixture until smooth. On low speed, fold in sour cream. Pour into crumb crust. Chill until set, but not firm. Then carefully spoon on pineapple-gelatin mixture. Chill until firm.

STRAWBERRY SHORTCAKE

Yield: Serves 6

2 cups sifted all-purpose flour
1 tablespoon baking powder
¾ teaspoons salt
¼ cup granulated sugar
½ cup shortening

1 egg
⅓ cup plus 1 tablespoon milk
2 pints strawberries, crushed and
  sweetened
½ quart heavy cream, chilled

Clean strawberries, mash lightly, sweeten. Save a few pretty ones for garnish. Set oven at 450° F. to preheat. Sift flour, baking powder, salt and sugar into large mixer bowl. Add shortening. Put egg into small mixer bowl. Beat on high speed for 10 seconds. Turn to low speed. Add milk and stir for a few seconds. Remove from mixer. Blend shortening and flour on low speed until like cornmeal, then add milk mixture. Beat only until blended. Pat dough into greased 9-inch round layer pan. Bake about 15 minutes or until browned. Split shortcake, brush with melted butter. Put strawberries between layers and on top. Pile on the whipped cream or pass the cream pitcher. Garnish with whole berries.

Note: Other fruits such as sliced, sweetened peaches, raspberries, etc., can be used. Also packaged cake mix or other plain or sponge cake can be used as a base.

BAKED ALASKA

Yield: 12 servings

1 9 x 9 x 2-inch layer of cake
1 quart ice cream
4 egg whites

½ teaspoon cream of tartar
⅔ cup light brown sugar (packed)

Prepare cake and set aside 1 layer for this dessert. Use any flavor desired: Devils food cake looks nice with chocolate chip ice cream, yellow cake with strawberry.

Cover baking sheet with aluminum foil. Place the cooled cake on baking sheet. Place solid brick of ice cream on cake, or pile ice cream on cake and cut away cake to shape of ice cream. Leave a 1-inch edge of cake all around. Freeze the cake and ice cream.

Preheat oven to 500° F. Adjust shelf in oven to lowest position. Beat egg whites and cream of tartar until foamy. Beat in brown sugar, 1 tablespoon at a time; continue beating until stiff and glossy. Remove cake and ice cream from freezer. Completely cover both cake and ice cream with the meringue, sealing it to the foil. If desired, you can freeze the entire dessert now for up to 24 hours.

Bake cake on lowest rack in oven 3-5 minutes or until meringue is light brown. Trim foil and transfer cake to serving plate. Cut and serve immediately.

WHIPPED CREAM CHEESE CAKE   Yield: 16 servings

3 (8 ounce) cartons whipped cream
   cheese
1 cup granulated sugar
1 teaspoon salt
¼ cup sifted all-purpose flour
5 eggs, separated
3 tablespoons lemon juice

¼ teaspoon nutmeg
1 teaspoon vanilla extract
½ teaspoon almond extract
1 cup sour cream
¼ cup granulated sugar
Graham Cracker pie crust (see
   Crumb Crusts)

Preheat oven to 325° F. Press pie crust on bottom and sides of 10-inch springform
pan. Chill. In large mixer bowl combine the cream cheese, sugar and salt and mix
well at low speed. Add flour and egg yolks and beat thoroughly. On low speed stir
in lemon juice, nutmeg, vanilla and almond extracts and the sour cream. Wash
beaters. In separate bowl at high speed beat the egg whites with ¼ cup sugar until
stiff peaks form. Fold into cheese mixture, blending thoroughly. Pour the mixture
into chilled pie crust and bake 1 hour. Cool in the oven for 1 hour; cool on rack
then refrigerate until well chilled. Do not remove outer rim of pan till ready to
serve.

ANGEL CAKE SURPRISE   Yield: 8-10 servings

1 (9-inch) Angel Cake
1 tablespoon (1 package) unflavored
   gelatin
¼ cup cold water

1 (12 ounce) box frozen sliced
   strawberries (or you can substitute
   raspberries or chopped, peeled
   peaches)
1 tablespoon lemon juice
1½ cups heavy cream

Chill cake. Cut off a slice ¾-inch thick from the top of the cake and set aside. Remove center of the cake with a fork, leaving about ¾-inches of cake on bottom and
sides. You will have a tunnel going around the cake. Tear up the insides of the
cake with a fork and reserve. Soften gelatin in water and dissolve over hot water.
Add to the defrosted strawberries along with the lemon juice. Chill until slightly
thickened. Pour ½ cup cream into small mixer bowl and place in refrigerator, with
beaters, to chill thoroughly. At high speed, whip cream until stiff. Fold cream and
cake crumbs into strawberry mixture. Fill the cake cavity with this mixture. Replace the top slice of cake. Wrap in aluminum foil or plastic wrap and chill
thoroughly. Before serving, whip remaining cup of cream, sweetening to taste,
and frost entire cake with whipped cream.

APRICOT SHORTCAKE Yield: 6-8 servings

Vanilla wafers or 1 package Lady
  Fingers
1 cup dried apricots
2½ cups water
1 envelope (1 tablespoon) plain
  unflavored gelatin
¼ cup granulated sugar
2 tablespoons apricot or orange
  liqueur (optional)

1 envelope (1 tablespoon) plain
  unflavored gelatin
¼ cup cold water
1 egg
1 cup whipping cream
¼ cup granulated sugar
1 teaspoon vanilla extract

Cover bottom of a 9-inch loaf pan with vanilla wafers, or arrange Lady Fingers, split in half, on bottom and along sides of loaf pan. Slowly cook apricots in water until very soft and broken up. Mash with the back of a wooden spoon. Add the gelatin and sugar and stir to dissolve. Stir in liqueur and set aside to cool. When cool, pour over wafers in loaf pan. Sprinkle second tablespoon gelatin over cold water to soften, using a heat-proof cup. Place cup in pan of hot water and stir to dissolve gelatin. Remove cup from water to cool gelatin slightly (but not enough to solidify). Beat egg thoroughly at high speed till it thickens and lightens in color. Set aside. Whip chilled cream, adding sugar and vanilla. When cream thickens, beat in gelatin, then, at low speed, fold in egg. Pour cream mixture over the apricot layer. Refrigerate at least 4 hours before serving.

LEMON CREAM TORTE Yield: 4-6 servings

4 egg whites
1 cup granulated sugar
½ teaspoon vanilla extract
4 egg yolks
¾ cup granulated sugar

3 tablespoons lemon juice
2 teaspoons grated lemon rind
½ cup heavy cream
2 teaspoons vanilla extract

Preheat oven to 250° F. Cover a cookie sheet with brown paper and draw two 8-inch circles on it (trace around the bottom of an 8-inch cake pan). Grease the paper thoroughly and sprinkle with flour. Beat egg whites to soft peak, then add ⅔ cup sugar gradually, beating well. Add vanilla then sprinkle in remaining sugar and mix or fold till meringue is smooth. It should hold very stiff points. Spoon half the meringue onto one circle (about ¾-inch thick), and remaining meringue onto second circle. Smooth out so it is of even thickness. Bake about 60 minutes, or until slightly golden and surface is hard to the touch. Cool, then remove gently from paper to a platter using a spatula.

For the filling, beat the 4 egg yolks with ½ cup sugar until smooth. Add lemon juice and rind and cook over very low heat, stirring constantly, until smooth and very thick. Do not allow it to boil. Total cooking time should be about 10 minutes. Cool. Whip the cream until it holds a point, then beat in remaining ¼ cup sugar and the vanilla. Fold in the cooled lemon sauce very carefully. Refrigerate.

To serve: Place a circle of meringue on a serving plate, cover with half the lemon sauce; place second meringue over this, and spoon on remaining lemon sauce. Cut into wedges to serve.

VIENNESE CHOCOLATE MERINGUE   Yield: 6-8 servings

3 egg whites
¼ teaspoon cream of tartar
⅛ teaspoon salt
¾ cup granulated sugar
2 cups (12 ounces) semisweet
   chocolate bits

1 tablespoon instant coffee
¼ cup boiling water
1 cup heavy cream
1 teaspoon vanilla extract

Grease bottom and sides of an 8-inch pie pan. Preheat oven to 275° F. Beat egg whites until they stand in soft peaks. Sprinkle in cream of tartar and salt. Add sugar gradually and continue beating until stiff, precise points come up. Spread about ⅔ of the meringue on the bottom of pie pan. Use remaining meringue to cover sides and mound around rim of pan. Bake 1 hour until delicately gold.

FILLING

Melt chocolate over hot water. Stir in coffee and boiling water. Beat by hand until very creamy and slightly cool. Beat the cream until stiff and mix or fold into chocolate mixture gently. Add vanilla extract and pour into the cool meringue shell. Chill several hours.

GRAND MARNIER SOUFFLE   Yield: 10-12 servings

¾ cup granulated sugar
3 envelopes (3 tablespoons)
   unflavored gelatin
1¼ cups milk
8 egg yolks, slightly beaten
1¼ cups orange juice

1½ tablespoons grated orange rind
8 egg whites
¾ teaspoon cream of tartar
¾ cup granulated sugar
½ cup Grand Marnier
1½ cups heavy cream, whipped

Separate eggs, then be sure to let them sit at room temperature till warmed. Using a 26-inch piece of waxed paper, make a collar for a 2-quart soufflé dish. Fold the waxed paper in half and secure it around the dish with tape. It should form a 2-inch rim above the top edge.

In a medium saucepan, combine the ¾ cup sugar with gelatin, milk and yolks. Stirring constantly, cook over medium heat until mixture thickens and reaches boiling stage, but do not allow it to boil; it will curdle. Immediately remove from heat and cool. Put mixture into a large bowl, add orange juice and rind and refrigerate until it thickens and mounds slightly when lifted with a spoon. With mixer at high speed, beat egg whites with cream of tartar until soft peaks form. By hand, with a rubber scraper, gently fold the whites into the chilled orange mixture. Then fold in Grand Marnier and whipped cream. Spoon into prepared soufflé dish and chill in refrigerator at least 4 hours. Before serving, very carefully peel off the waxed paper collar. Garnish with whipped cream piped out of a star-tipped pastry tube, and add pieces of unpeeled orange.

PAVLOVA   Yield: 8 servings

6 egg whites
1½ teaspoons cream of tartar
¼ teaspoon salt
1½ cups granulated sugar

1 teaspoon vanilla extract
1 cup heavy cream, whipped
2 cups fresh or canned and drained
   berries or fruit*

Preheat oven to 250° F. Allow egg whites to warm to room temperature. Beat at high speed until frothy; add cream of tartar and salt. Beat until stiff peaks form; gradually beat in granulated sugar, 2 tablespoons at a time. Add vanilla and continue beating until very stiff — it should be beaten enough to dissolve the sugar. Place a piece of aluminum foil on a cookie sheet. Using a cake pan as a guide, draw a 9-inch circle on the foil. Grease thoroughly. Pile about a third of the meringue on the circle and smooth out to cover the circle making a layer about ¼-inch thick. Fill a pastry bag fitted with a 1-inch decorative nozzle, with remaining meringue and pipe it around the edge of the circle in decorative swirls, to form a case.

Bake in preheated oven about 1¼ hours. Turn off heat and leave in oven about 30 minutes. Cool completely. When cold, place on serving plate. Spoon whipped cream into center; pile on the sliced fruit.

* Note: Usually this is topped with berries. Use 1½ cups washed berries placed on top of the whipped cream. Crush ½ cup berries and add just a bit of sugar; pour over top of dessert.
Or: Try other fruits in season. A beautiful presentation is made with sliced Kiwi fruit topping the cream.

MERINGUES GLACE MELBA   Yield: 6 servings

3 egg whites
⅛ teaspoon salt
½ teaspoon cider vinegar
1 cup granulated sugar

½ teaspoon vanilla extract
1 quart vanilla ice cream
18 canned, frozen, or sweetened
   fresh peach slices

Preheat oven to 300° F. Cover a baking sheet with brown paper. Add salt and vinegar to egg whites, beat until frothy throughout. Add sugar gradually, beating after each addition until all has been added. This should take 5-10 minutes. Add vanilla. Divide meringue into 6 portions; drop onto paper. Make a shallow depression in each, so that you have shallow bowl-shaped meringues. Bake about 40 minutes, or until they begin to brown. Remove from oven; remove from paper immediately; cool.

To serve: Arrange 3 peach slices in bottom of each shell, top with scoop of ice cream and garnish with raspberry sauce.

RASPBERRY SAUCE

1 package (10 ounce) frozen raspberries, defrosted
2 teaspoons cornstarch

Drain juice from defrosted raspberries, adding enough water, if necessary to make ¾ cup. Blend cornstarch with small amount of juice and combine with remaining juice in small saucepan. Cook and stir until clear and thickened; fold in drained berries. Cool.

KORITZ ARBUSH DESSERT   Yield: 6-8 servings

An Armenian favorite.

2 tablespoons butter
⅓ cup all-purpose flour
3 egg whites
⅔ cup brown sugar
⅔ cup confectioners' sugar

½ cup granulated sugar
1½ teaspoons vanilla extract
½ teaspoon cloves
½ teaspoon cinnamon
1¼ cups finely chopped walnuts

Topping

1 cup heavy cream
½ teaspoon vanilla extract

1 tablespoon granulated sugar
1 banana, sliced

Preheat oven to 350° F. Grease thoroughly an 8-inch pie pan.

Melt the butter in a saucepan; stir in flour and cook on low heat about 10 minutes or until golden brown. Stir constantly. Cool to lukewarm. Beat the egg whites until stiff; beat in the sugars very gradually, then beat in vanilla and spices. At low speed, stir in the cooled flour-butter mixture and the walnuts. Spread into well-greased pie pan. Bake 20 minutes or until golden brown. Turn off the oven and keep the dessert in the closed oven for 5 more minutes. Remove from oven and cool.

To serve: whip the cream till stiff, adding the vanilla and sugar. Spread over the dessert; garnish with the sliced banana.

CHOCOLATE SOUFFLE

Yield: 4-6 servings

Serve a light main course with this.

2 squares (2 ounces) unsweetened
   chocolate
¼ cup butter
¼ cup all-purpose flour
1¼ cups milk
¼ teaspoon salt

5 egg yolks
1 teaspoon vanilla extract
1 tablespoon brandy
⅔ cup granulated sugar
6 egg whites

Sweetened whipped cream
Hot fudge sauce

Melt chocolate and set aside. Melt butter in a saucepan and stir in the flour. Add milk and stir constantly until mixture comes to a boil. Stir in the salt. Beat the egg yolks lightly in a small bowl, adding vanilla and brandy. Gradually, beat in the hot cream sauce. Add melted chocolate and beat thoroughly.

Note that this much of the soufflé can be prepared ahead of time. Cover the bowl with plastic wrap and set aside. Do not refrigerate. Grease a 1½-quart casserole or soufflé dish. Fold a 26-inch piece of waxed paper in half, grease it, and wrap around the outside of the dish to form a collar. Fasten with tape or string. Preheat oven to 375° F. Beat egg whites until just stiff, then very gradually beat in the sugar. Do not overbeat. Stir a large spoonful of the egg white mixture into the chocolate base and mix in thoroughly. Now fold the remaining egg white into the chocolate mixture, using as few strokes as possible (a few white streaks of egg white won't matter at all). Pour into prepared dish and bake about 45 minutes. Serve AT ONCE with sweetened whipped cream and hot fudge sauce.

Note: Time this so that your guests wait for it — don't let the soufflé wait, for it won't!

LEMON ICE   Yield: 8 servings

2 cups granulated sugar
4 cups water

1 cup lemon juice
1 tablespoon grated lemon rind

Use fresh lemon juice, juicing lemons with your mixer juicer attachment. Cook water and sugar together for about 5 minutes; cool. Stir in lemon juice and grated lemon rind. Freeze to a mush. Break up into mixer bowl, beat well at medium speed to break up all ice crystals; freeze again till firm. Keep covered in freezer. This makes a refreshing snack, dessert, or serve it on a fresh fruit salad.

LEMON ICE CREAM   Yield: 6 servings

1 cup milk
1 cup cream
1 cup granulated sugar

Grated rind of 2 lemons
½ cup lemon juice

Using the juicer attachment on your mixer, juice fresh lemons to obtain ½ cup lemon juice. Combine milk, cream and sugar and heat over low heat, stirring until sugar is dissolved. Cool slightly, then combine with lemon rind and lemon juice. Freeze to a mush. Whip at high speed till fluffy and all ice crystals are broken up. Freeze again. Store tightly covered in freezer.

ORANGE ICE   Yield: 4-6 servings

2 cups water
1 cup granulated sugar
¼ cup freshly squeezed orange juice

¼ cup freshly sqeezed lemon juice
⅛ teaspoon salt
1 tablespoon grated orange rind

Use the juicer attachment on your mixer to juice oranges and lemons. Using a hand grater, grate peel of orange before juicing to obtain the 1 tablespoon orange rind.

Simmer water and sugar 5 minutes. Remove from heat and stir in remaining ingredients. Freeze to a mush, 1½-2 hours. Break up into large mixer bowl. Beat at high speed till all ice crystals are broken up. Freeze. Store covered in freezer.

APRICOT NOODLE PUDDING

Yield: 6 servings

Apricot Kugel

8 ounces medium noodles
⅔ cup dried apricots
3 eggs
1 cup large curd cottage cheese
½ cup sour cream
3 tablespoons melted butter
  or margarine
3 tablespoons granulated sugar

1½ teaspoons vanilla extract
1 teaspoon ground cinnamon
¼ teaspoon ground nutmeg
1 teaspoon grated lemon rind
¼ teaspoon salt
1 cup fresh bread crumbs
⅓ cup finely chopped walnuts or
  almonds

Cook noodles in a large amount of water until just done. Drain and rinse with cold water.

Preheat oven to 375° F. Grease an 8 x 8 x 2-inch baking pan. Cover apricots with boiling water; let stand for 15 minutes; drain and chop fine. In a bowl, beat the eggs thoroughly. At low speed, stir in cottage cheese, sour cream, 1 tablespoon of the melted butter, sugar, vanilla, cinnamon, nutmeg, lemon rind, salt and apricots. By hand, gently stir in the noodles. In a small skillet, gently toast the bread crumbs and nuts in the 2 tablespoons melted butter. Sprinkle over noodles. Bake 30 minutes till golden brown.

CHEESECAKE DELIGHT

Yield: 10-12 servings

1 9-inch Graham Cracker Pie Crust
11 ounces cream cheese
2 eggs
½ cup granulated sugar

1½ teaspoons vanilla extract
2 cups sour cream
¼ cup granulated sugar

Refrigerate crust while making filling. Preheat oven to 375° F. Place cream cheese in large mixing bowl; cream at low speed; add eggs, one at a time, beating at medium speed after each addition. Continue beating the filling at low speed, gradually adding sugar and vanilla. Pour into crust and bake 20 minutes. At low speed, blend sour cream with sugar and spread mixture over top of pie. Turn off the oven heat. Return pie to oven and bake 5 minutes. Cool then chill. Garnish with sliced strawberries if desired.

Chapter Eight
GOOD MIXERS
(Party Meals and Menus)

MAKING MEMORABLE MENUS

Good parties don't just happen. Careful planning, good food, and the right people — good mixers — are the important ingredients. Today's hosts and hostesses want as little fuss and bother as possible, and with the help of modern kitchen appliances, it's easy and fun to entertain. Keep these pointers in mind when you're planning your menus:

— Have a variety of flavors — not all bland or spicy, sweet or sour.

— Mix, don't match, when it come to textures of food. For instance, serve a crisp salad (page 120) with Cheese Soufflé (page 109) a crunchy cookie (pages 72-85) with smooth ice cream (page 139).

— Add little touches to create color and interest. Take advantage of the range of hues found in foods to make a plate that's eye-appealing. Red Pepper Jam (page 123) will add color to the cocktail or relish tray. A sprig of parsley, spiced crabapple or lemon wedge can brighten up a platter.

— Sometimes just a spoonful of whipped cream will help. To have it ready: Whip cream and sweeten it. Drop spoonfuls on a cookie sheet and freeze. Put these frozen mounds of cream in a plastic bag and keep them in the freezer, ready to use whenever needed.

— For nutritional balance, you need some protein — Liver Loaf (page 104), Salmon Mousse (page 104), or Cheese Strata (page 113), for instance. Include vegetables and fruits such as Brocolli Soufflé (page 116), Carrot Mold (page 116) and fresh fruits with Creamy Fruit Dressing (page 126). Serve wonderful homemade breads (pages 24-48) for the pleasure of it and the "good for you" grains, and there you have it — well-balanced menus.

— Spicy snacks before meals help stimulate appetites. Put them in the living room where guests can help themselves while you take care of last minute touches on dinner.

— A lovely bowl of fruit can double as a centerpiece and dessert.

— Use flowers and candles to create a festive atmosphere.

— Experiment with new foods and ideas to create excitement with your meals.

— Do your marketing, prepare and freeze dishes well in advance; try to leave as little as possible for the last minute.

MENUS AND RECIPES

The following are some suggested menus and recipes for parties. There are many other recipes in this cookbook you will find suitable for entertaining. You may wish to substitute the Coconut Birthday Cake (page 56), the Chocolate Soufflé (page 138), the Breast of Chicken Normandy (page 103), or others depending on the occasion.

Dinner
Curry Dip with Raw Vegetables
Beef Vegetable Casserole
Cabbage Slaw   Dill Bread
Sponge Cake with Lemon Sauce
Chocolate Ice Cream

CURRY DIP   Yield: 2 cups

1 package (8 ounces) Cream cheese,
    softened
2-3 teaspoons curry powder
1 teaspoon onion powder

½ teaspoon seasoned salt
1 tablespoon snipped parsley
1 cup dairy sour cream
Fresh vegetables for dipping

In small bowl combine cream cheese and seasonings. Blend at low speed until very smooth. Gradually beat in sour cream and parsley. Cover and chill to blend flavors. Serve with carrot sticks, zucchini sticks, fresh mushrooms, celery, green beans — just about any raw vegetable you like.

BEEF AND VEGETABLE CASSEROLE   Yield: 12 servings

2 medium onions, chopped
2 pounds ground beef
Salt and pepper to taste
2 cans (5 cups) or 1 pound
    cooked green beans
2 (10½ or 11-ounce) cans condensed
    tomato soup

10 medium potatoes, cooked
1 cup warm milk
2 beaten eggs
Salt and pepper

Preheat oven to 350° F. Cook onion in hot fat until golden; add meat and seasonings; brown. Add drained beans and soup; pour into greased 3-quart casserole. With electric mixer, mash the potatoes; beat in the milk, eggs and seasonings until light and fluffy. Spoon in mounds over meat. Bake 30-45 minutes.

CABBAGE SLAW   Yield: 12 servings

6 cups shredded cabbage
  (1 medium head)
4 tablespoons minced onion
½ cup granulated sugar
1½ teaspoons salt

½ teaspoon dry mustard
½ teaspoon celery seed
½ cup white vinegar
½ cup salad oil

Using the slicer attachment on your mixer, finely chop the cabbage. Toss with onion and sugar. Combine remaining ingredients in a saucepan. Stirring often, bring to a boil. Pour at once over the cabbage, mixing thoroughly. Cover tightly and chill thoroughly, at least 4 hours. This salad keeps well in the refrigerator as long as 6 days.

DILL BREAD   Yield: 1 loaf or 36 rolls

1 cup creamed cottage cheese
1 package active dry yeast
¼ cup warm water (115-120° F.)
2 tablespoons granulated sugar
1 tablespoon minced onion
1 tablespoon butter or margarine

2 teaspoons dill seed
½ teaspoon salt
¼ teaspoon baking soda
1 egg, slightly beaten
2½-3 cups sifted all-purpose flour

Heat cottage cheese to lukewarm. Dissolve yeast in warm water and place in large mixer bowl along with cottage cheese, sugar, onion, butter or margarine, dill seed, salt, soda and egg. Insert dough hooks. Beat in flour to form a soft dough, mixing and kneading for 5-6 minutes. Cover bowl and put in warm place to rise until doubled, about 1 hour. Stir down the dough; turn into a well-greased 8-inch or 9-inch casserole. Let rise in warm place until light, 30-45 minutes. Preheat oven to 350° F. and bake 40-45 minutes, or until bread tests done. **Note:** to make Dill Rolls, fill muffin cups half full of dough. Allow to rise until double, and bake at 350° F. about 20 minutes.

SPONGE CAKE   Yield: 1 tube cake

6 egg whites
6 egg yolks
1½ cups sifted cake flour
½ teaspoon salt
1 teaspoon baking powder

1½ cups granulated sugar
½ teaspoon cream of tartar
½ cup cold water
1 teaspoon lemon extract
1 teaspoon vanilla extract

Preheat oven to 375° F. Separate eggs, let stand at room temperature for 1 hour. Sift cake flour, salt, baking powder and 1 cup sugar. Combine in large mixing bowl, egg whites and cream of tartar. Beat for 2 minutes on medium speed until egg whites hold soft peaks. Gradually beat in ½ cup sugar on medium speed for 2 minutes. In small mixing bowl, combine egg yolks, water, lemon and vanilla extract. Add dry ingredients. Blend on low speed for 1 minute. Pour batter into ungreased 10 x 4-inch tube pan. Bake at 375° F. for 35-40 minutes — until toothpick inserted into center comes out clean. Invert cake on small neck bottle or inverted funnel until cake is completely cooled. Remove from pan.

Suggested Topping:

LEMON SAUCE   Yield: ⅔ cup

2 teaspoons margarine
1½ cups confectioners' sugar
¼ cup lemon juice

Combine margarine, sugar and lemon juice in a saucepan. Heat over low heat until completely dissolved. Set aside to cool. Drizzle over cake.

CHOCOLATE ICE CREAM   Yield: 1½ quarts

4 cups milk
3 ounces (3 squares) unsweetened
   chocolate
1 cup granulated sugar
1 tablespoon all-purpose flour
¼ teaspoon salt

2 eggs
1 envelope unflavored gelatin
¼ cup cold water
2 teaspoons vanilla extract
1 cup heavy cream

Pour half of milk into saucepan; add chocolate; heat until melted. Stir together half of sugar with the flour and salt; add hot milk, stirring well. Return to saucepan; cook for 10 minutes, stirring frequently. Beat eggs; beat in remaining sugar and milk. Add to hot mixture. Stir in gelatin which has been softened in water. Cook until the custard coats a silver spoon. Remove from heat and cool thoroughly. Freeze in refrigerator trays. When partially frozen, beat well; add vanilla. Whip cream and fold in. Freeze.

Supper

Egg Spread on Crackers
Ravioli   Tossed Green Salad with Dressing (page 125)
Macaroon Supreme Pies   Vanilla Ice Cream

EGG SPREAD   Yield: 2 cups

1 package (8 ounce) cream cheese
¼ cup mayonnaise
2 tablespoons minced onion
¼ teaspoon freshly ground black
  pepper

1 (4-ounce) jar or can chopped pimiento-
  stuffed green olives, or chopped
  black olives, or chopped pimiento
2 large hard-cooked eggs

Be sure to have cream cheese at room temperature. Beat at low speed, gradually beating in mayonnaise, onion and black pepper. Drain olives or pimiento and beat them in. By hand, stir in chopped eggs. If you do not like the flavor of olives, add extra hard-cooked egg. Serve on crackers, or as a dip.

RAVIOLI   Yield: 36 ravioli

Dough
3 cups all-purpose flour
4 eggs
1 tablespoon salt

Insert dough hooks. Combine all ingredients in mixer bowl. Beat on medium speed about 5 minutes, on low speed 2 minutes. The dough should form a ball and be smooth and elastic. Divide dough into 6 parts. Cover each with plastic wrap. Allow to rest 30 minutes while you prepare the filling.

Roll out one ball to 13 x 5-inch rectangle, about ⅛-inch thick. Cover the rolled pasta with a damp towel to prevent its drying out, and roll out a second ball of dough to a similar size and shape. Place mounds of ravioli filling by rounded teaspoonfuls in 2 rows of 6 mounds each about 2-inches apart. Dip a pastry brush or your index finger in a bowl of water and make lines of water between the mounds (the water will help hold the finished ravioli together). Roll out another sheet of pasta to same measurement and carefully place on top of the first one, pressing down firmly around the filling and along the wetted lines. With a pastry cutter or a small, sharp knife, cut into squares along the wetted line. Separate the mounds of ravioli and set them aside on waxed paper. Follow the same procedure for the other 4 portions of dough.

To cook, drop the ravioli into 6 to 8 quarts of rapidly boiling salted water and stir them gently with a wooden spoon, to keep them from sticking to one another or the bottom of the pot. Boil the ravioli for about 8 minutes, then drain them thoroughly in a large colander. Serve the ravioli with tomato sauce or add butter and sprinkle with grated Parmesan cheese. Gently stir them all together immediately before serving.

RAVIOLI FILLINGS

Chicken or Turkey

2 cups cooked poultry
2 eggs
1 tablespoon soft butter
1 tablespoon all-purpose flour
½ cup light cream

½ teaspoon salt
⅛ teaspoon pepper
⅛ teaspoon nutmeg
1 cup grated Parmesan cheese

Using finest blade of your grinder attachment, grind 2 cups of poultry meat. Beat eggs and add butter, flour, cream, and seasonings. Beat in ground poultry, and cheese.

Cheese

1 pound ricotta or small curd cottage
  cheese
2 eggs

2 tablespoons Parmesan Cheese
Salt and pepper to taste

Beat all together thoroughly.

Beef

1 cup ground cooked beef
1 cup ground cooked pork
½ cup finely chopped Italian ham
3 tablespoons finely chopped fresh
  .parsley

2 eggs
½ cup grated Parmesan cheese
Salt and pepper to taste

Use finest blade of grinder attachment to grind beef and pork. Beat eggs thoroughly. Stir in remaining ingredients.

TOMATO SAUCE   Yield: 2 cups

2 tablespoons cooking oil
2 onions
2 cups Italian plum tomatoes
3 tablespoons tomato paste
1 tablespoon finely cut fresh basil
  or 2 teaspoons dried basil

1 teaspoon granulated sugar
½ teaspoon salt
Freshly ground black pepper

Chop onions and tomatoes using the coarse blade of the grinder attachment. In a 2 to 3-quart saucepan, heat the oil, add the onions and cook them over moderate heat until they are soft but not browned. Add remaining ingredients. Reduce the heat to very low and simmer with the pan partially covered, for abut 40 minutes. Stir occasionally. Serve hot.

MACAROON SUPREME PIES   Yield: 12-14 servings

6 eggs, separated
2 cups granulated sugar
2 cups graham cracker crumbs

2 cups finely chopped walnuts
2 teaspoons almond extract

Butter generously two 9-inch pie plates. Preheat oven to 350° F. Beat egg whites at high speed until soft peaks form; gradually beat in 1 cup sugar, beating until stiff peaks form. Beat egg yolks, adding 1 cup sugar, until light and very thick; stir in crumbs, nuts, and almond extract. Fold in egg whites. Pile into prepared pans. Bake 25 minutes. Serve cool with softened vanilla ice cream. Be sure not to over-cook; it will be chewy like macaroons. As it cools it wrinkles up and looses its puffiness.

VANILLA ICE CREAM   Yield: 1½ quarts

4 cups milk
1 package (3-ounce) regular
   vanilla pudding
1 cup light corn syrup

1 teaspoon vanilla extract
1 teaspoon almond extract
1 cup heavy cream

Gradually stir milk into pudding powder. Add corn syrup and mix until smooth. Cook over low heat until thickened, stirring constantly. Cool. Freeze in re-frigerator trays. When frozen about 1-inch thick around edges of the trays, put into large bowl and beat thoroughly. Add flavoring. Whip the cream and fold that into frozen mixture. Pour into trays and freeze till firm.

Open House

Cheddar Blue Cheese Ball   Spinach Squares
Mushroom Pastries   Tuna Butter
Marinated Carrots   Sweet and Sour Meatballs
Ratatouille   Cranberry Relish
Tempura
Meringue Cake   Lemon Tea Squares

CHEDDAR-BLEU CHEESE BALL   Yield: 1 large cheese ball

1 (5 ounce) jar sharp Cheddar cheese
   spread
½ (5 ounce) jar bleu cheese spread
1 (8 ounce) package cream cheese

1½ tablespoons wine vinegar
Dash garlic powder
½ pound bacon

Be sure all ingredients are at room temperature; put everything except bacon into a bowl and beat at medium speed until thoroughly combined. Refrigerate while preparing bacon. Cook bacon until crisp; drain thoroughly and crumble. Form a ball with the cream cheese mixture and roll in the bacon till thoroughly covered. Chill overnight.

SPINACH SQUARES   Yield: 40-60 squares

4 tablespoons butter or margarine
3 eggs
1 cup all-purpose flour
1 teaspoon salt
1 teaspoon baking powder
1 cup milk
½ pound medium sharp cheese,
   grated

½ pound sharp Cheddar cheese,
   grated
2 (10 ounce) packages frozen chopped
   spinach, thawed and squeezed dry
1 tablespoon finely chopped onion
Paprika

Preheat oven to 350° F. Put butter or margarine in 13 x 9 x 2-inch pan and place in oven to melt. Remove from oven and allow to cool. In large mixer bowl beat eggs well, using medium speed. At low speed, stir in flour, salt, baking powder and milk. Mix well. By hand, add melted butter or margarine, cheeses, spinach, onion, and mix well. Spoon into baking pan and level off. Sprinkle with paprika. Bake at 350° F. for 45-50 minutes. Allow to cool for 45 minutes, then cut into bite-size squares, ¾ to 1-inch each.

Note: Spinach Squares freeze well. Place squares on cookie sheet and put into freezer until frozen solid. They can then be transferred to an airtight freezer bag or container. To serve, reheat at 325° F. for 12-15 minutes.

MUSHROOM PASTRIES   Yield: Lots

Well worth the trouble — these will become your favorite appetizers!

PASTRY

3 (3 ounce) packages cream cheese
½ cup butter
1½ cups sifted all-purpose flour

Cream together thoroughly at medium speed the cream cheese and butter. Insert dough hooks and gradually add the flour. The dough should form a ball. Flatten the ball, wrap in waxed paper and refrigerate for at least 2 hours.

MUSHROOM FILLING

¼ pound fresh mushrooms, finely chopped
2 tablespoons butter
½ small onion, finely chopped
⅛ teaspoon thyme

¼ teaspoon salt
⅛ teaspoon pepper
1½ tablespoons all-purpose flour
½ cup dairy sour cream

Melt butter and sauté the chopped onion until just lightly browned. Add the chopped mushrooms, thyme, salt, pepper, and cook about 5 minutes, stirring frequently. Sprinkle with flour and stir and cook for a minute. Reduce heat; stir in sour cream. Cook, stirring constantly, until thickened. Cool, then chill thoroughly.

Roll out pastry to about ⅛-inch thickness. Cut into 3-inch rounds. Place ½ teaspoon filling on each round, wet the edges, fold over and crimp edges with a fork. Prick the top with a fork to allow steam to escape when baking. Chill. Bake in a preheated 450° F. oven about 15 minutes, till lightly browned. If frozen, they will need a couple of extra minutes in the oven.

These can be made ahead and refrigerated, then baked. Or, layer on a cookie sheet and freeze. When frozen solid, carefully pack them in a plastic bag or a box and store in the freezer. Allow to defrost a few minutes before baking.

TUNA BUTTER   Yield: Approximately 3 cups

2 cans (6½ or 7 ounces each) tuna in vegetable oil
8 ounces salted whipped butter or 1 cup soft butter or margarine
¼ cup minced parsley

1 tablespoon finely chopped onion
¼ teaspoon dried dill weed
½ teaspoon grated lemon rind
1 teaspoon lemon juice

In medium bowl, break tuna into fine flakes. Add remaining ingredients and beat well. Turn into small crock or serving bowl. Cover and chill. Allow to stand at room temperature for 15-30 minutes before serving. Set out on a platter with melba toast, crisp crackers or cocktail bread slices.

MARINATED CARROTS   Yield: 10 servings

Use as a cold vegetable dish or as a relish.

2 pounds carrots
1 can tomato soup
1 cup granulated sugar
½ cup vegetable oil
½ cup white wine vinegar

1 teaspoon dried mustard
½ teaspoon salt
¼ teaspoon pepper
1 green pepper, diced
1 large onion, diced

Wash and scrape carrots. Using the slicer attachment on your mixer, thinly slice all carrots. Cook until done (be careful not to overcook — a bit underdone is best). Drain.

Combine all remaining ingredients and stir over medium heat to dissolve sugar. Pour this hot mixture over the drained, cooked carrots. Put into large refrigerator container and refrigerate 24 hours.

SWEET AND SOUR MEATBALLS   Yield: 12 servings

½ cup chopped onion
2 tablespoons butter or margarine
2 pounds ground beef
1 teaspoon salt
½ teaspoon ground pepper

½ cup all-purpose flour
2 eggs
½ cup light cream
2 cans condensed consommé

Cook onion in butter until tender but not brown. In mixer bowl, combine meat and seasonings. Insert dough hooks and beat at medium speed. At low speed, beat in flour, then egg. Gradually beat in cream. Add onion. The mixture should be light and fluffy.

Form mixture into 1-inch balls and place in large baking pan. Cover with Sweet-Sour Sauce and bake at 350° F. for 45-60 minutes. When done, skim off fat and thicken sauce using 2-3 tablespoons flour mixed into a paste with water.

Sweet-Sour Sauce

¾ cup brown sugar
1 can undiluted consommé

½ cup cider vinegar
½ teaspoon dry mustard

Combine and pour over uncooked meatballs.

RATATOUILLE   Yield: 12 servings

½ cup olive oil
4 cloves garlic, peeled and chopped
2 large onions, sliced

1 large eggplant
4 zucchini, sliced
¼ cup all-purpose flour (optional)

4 green peppers, seeded and cut
  into strips
6 large ripe tomatoes, peeled and
  sliced
  or 2 1-pound cans sliced tomatoes
Salt and freshly ground black pepper

Using the slicer attachment, slice onion and garlic. Cut each pepper into fourths, and put them through the slicer also, to cut strips.

Sauté garlic and onion in olive oil just until onion is transparent. Peel and cube the eggplant. Put sliced squash and eggplant into a bag with the flour and shake to coat the vegetables. Put into skillet along with green pepper; cover and simmer, until thick. Season to taste with salt and pepper. Serve hot or cold. Without the flour, you have a jucier dish, a little lower in calories.

CRANBERRY ORANGE RELISH   Yield: 1 quart

1 pound fresh cranberries
2 oranges
2 cups granulated sugar

Wash cranberries and pick out any bad ones. Wash oranges; seed them and cut into chunks large enough to fit into the food chopper. Attach grinder attachment to mixer, using shredder blade. Grind cranberries and oranges. Stir in sugar thoroughly. Refrigerate. This freezes well.

TEMPURA

Japanese deep fried seafood and vegetables. The food is fried at the table, dipped in sauce, and served immediately. Use an electric wok, skillet or deep fryer.

Choose from these:

shrimps, shelled and cleaned
cubed fish fillets
chicken livers
mushrooms, sliced if large, whole if small
carrots, cut into thin diagonal slices
Snow peas
eggplant, cut into strips
green peppers, cut into cubes
broccoli flowerettes

Cut up, and be sure everything is dry. Using a slotted spoon or tongs, dip into one of the following batters. Have peanut oil heated to 350° F. Be sure not to have too much batter on food. Fry, turning to brown. Total frying time is usually 2-4 minutes. Drain thoroughly and serve with sauce, or plain soy sauce. Serve with plenty of rice.

BATTERS   Yield: 2 cups for all batters

Beer Tempura Batter

2 eggs
1⅓ cups sifted all-purpose flour

1 teaspoon salt
1 cup flat beer

Place eggs, flour and salt in a bowl and beat well, gradually adding beer. Beat until smooth. Let stand for 1 hour or refrigerate overnight.

Golden Tempura Batter

1 large egg
1 cup water
1¼ cups sifted all-purpose flour

Beat the egg and water together; add flour all at once and beat until smooth. Let stand at least 1 hour or refrigerate overnight.

Light Batter

1 cup sifted all-purpose flour
½ teaspoon baking powder
½ teaspoon salt

1 tablespoon vegetable oil
2 eggs separated
⅔ cup milk

Combine flour, baking powder, salt, oil, egg yolks and milk in a bowl. Beat until smooth. Let rest 1 hour. Beat whites until soft peaks form and fold into batter just before using.

DIPPING SAUCES FOR TEMPURA

Seafood Sauce   Yield: ¾ cup

½ cup chicken broth
2 tablespoons soy sauce

2 teaspoons granulated sugar
1 tablespoon horseradish

Combine and serve warm in dipping bowls.

Sauce for Chicken   Yield: 1 cup

½ cup chicken broth
4 tablespoons soy sauce
4 tablespoons sherry

Combine all ingredients and serve warm in dipping bowls.

Lemon Sauce   Yield: 1½ cups

1 cup cold chicken broth
2 tablespoons cornstarch
3 tablespoons lemon juice
½ teaspoon freshly grated ginger

2 tablespoons soy sauce
1 tablespoon honey or granulated
  sugar
2 teaspoons grated lemon rind

Combine in saucepan; stirring constantly. Bring to a boil. Serve in dipping bowls garnished with lemon slices.

Other Suggestions

Bottled Sweet-Sour Sauce
Hoisin Sauce
Bottled Plum Sauce

LEMON TEA SQUARES   Yield: About 117 one-inch squares

6 tablespoons butter or margarine
1 cup granulated sugar
2 eggs
1½ cups sifted all-purpose flour

1½ teaspoons baking powder
¼ teaspoon salt
½ cup milk
Grated rind of one lemon

GLAZE

⅔ cup granulated sugar
Juice of one lemon

Grease thoroughly a 13 x 9 x 2-inch pan. Preheat oven to 350° F. In mixer bowl at medium speed cream butter and sugar; beat in eggs, one at a time. At low speed, beat in flour, baking powder, salt, milk and lemon rind. Pour batter into prepared pan and bake 25 minutes. Mix together the sugar and lemon juice. Very carefully remove the cake from oven and spoon the lemon-sugar mixture over the top. Bake 5 more minutes. Cut while warm into 1-inch squares.

MERINGUE CAKE   Yield: 10-12 servings

A pretty cake.

Layers

1 cup sifted cake flour
1¼ teaspoons baking powder
⅛ teaspoon salt
½ cup butter or margarine

½ cup granulated sugar
4 egg yolks
¼ cup whole milk (or Half and Half)
½ teaspoon vanilla extract

Meringue

4 egg whites
⅛ teaspoon salt

1 cup granulated sugar
1 teaspoon vanilla extract
¼ cup chopped pecans or walnuts

Preheat oven to 350° F. Grease and flour two 9-inch layer pans. Sift together flour, baking powder and salt. Cream the butter or margarine with ½ cup sugar very thoroughly. Keep mixer at high speed and beat till very creamy; beat in egg yolks one at a time. Beat in milk and vanilla. Add dry ingredients and beat thoroughly for 2 minutes. Spread batter into prepared pans.

Beat the egg whites till stiff; add salt and 1 cup sugar gradually, in about four additions, then beat in the vanilla. Beat at least a minute after all sugar has been added. Spread the meringue over the two cake layers, much as you would for a meringue pie. It should be spread with swirls and peaks, and it should touch the sides of the pan and cover the cake completely. Sprinkle the nuts on one of the layers. Bake for 35 minutes, or until cakes test done with a toothpick. Let cool in pans.

To serve, remove layers from their pans. Place one layer meringue side down; the nut coated layer will go meringue side up. This can be served with a variety of fillings: Mash a pint of strawberries, saving a few nice berries for top garnish. Add sugar to taste, and put strawberries between the two layers. Or fold crushed strawberries into 1 cup heavy cream, whipped.

Lemon filling is delicious, or cook a half pound of dried apricots for about 25 minutes; mash thoroughly and sweeten to taste. Cool; fold into 1 cup heavy cream and pile between the two layers. Be sure to keep cake refrigerated.

Large Apple Turnover   Tea Doughnuts
Coffee

LARGE APPLE TURNOVER   Yield: 16-20 servings

12-14 apples
1¾ cups granulated sugar
2 teaspoons cinnamon
½ cup butter or margarine
1 egg

¾ teaspoon salt
4 teaspoons baking powder
¾ cup milk
2 cups all-purpose flour

Preheat oven to 350° F. Pare and core apples and slice into a 13 x 9 x 2-inch pan until you have a layer 1½-inches thick. Sprinkle with a mixture of 1 cup of the sugar and the cinnamon. Using mixer, cream remaining ¾ cup sugar and the butter or margarine. Beat in egg; blend well. At low speed, add combined salt, baking powder and flour alternately with the milk. Spoon over apples. Bake 30-40 minutes, or until nicely brown. Serve with lemon sauce, ice cream or whipped cream. Delicious plain, too.

TEA DOUGHNUTS   Yield: About 1 dozen

1 egg
½ cup milk
1 teaspoon vanilla extract
1⅓ cups sifted all-purpose flour
2 teaspoons baking powder

¼ teaspoon salt
⅓ cup granulated sugar
1 tablespoon melted shortening
Approximately 1 pound shortening
  for frying

Beat egg till foamy; beat in milk and vanilla. Sift together dry ingredients and blend together at low speed, just until combined. Stir in the melted shortening. Dip a teaspoon into hot shortening, to coat spoon, then dip up a spoonful of batter. Quickly immerse spoon into hot shortening (375° F.) and allow batter to drop off. Fry until brown, 3-5 minutes.

VARIATIONS

Pecan Doughnuts: Add ½ cup chopped pecans.
Orange Doughnuts: Add grated rind of 1 orange.
Spice Doughnuts: Add 1 teaspoon cinnamon.
Honey Doughnuts: Use ¼ cup honey in place of ⅓ cup granulated sugar and reduce milk to ⅓ cup.

INDEX